Should Robots Replace Teachers?

Digital Futures Series

Should Robots Replace Teachers?

AI and the Future of Education

NEIL SELWYN

polity

The right of Neil Selwyn to be identified as Author of this Work has been asserted in accordance with the UK Copyright, Designs and Patents Act 1988.

First published in 2019 by Polity Press

Polity Press
65 Bridge Street
Cambridge CB2 1UR, UK

Polity Press
101 Station Landing
Suite 300
Medford, MA 02155, USA

ISBN-13: 978-1-5095-2895-0
ISBN-13: 978-1-5095-2896-7(pb)

A catalogue record for this book is available from the British Library.

Library of Congress Cataloging-in-Publication Data

Names: Selwyn, Neil, author.
Title: Should robots replace teachers? : AI and the future of education /
   Neil Selwyn.
Description: Cambridge, UK : Medford, MA, USA : Polity Press, [2019] |
   Series: Digital futures | Includes bibliographical references and index.
Identifiers: LCCN 2019001774 (print) | LCCN 2019011944 (ebook) | ISBN
   9781509528981 (Epub) | ISBN 9781509528950 | ISBN 9781509528967 (pb)
Subjects: LCSH: Artificial intelligence--Educational applications. |
   Intelligent tutoring systems.
Classification: LCC LB1028.43 (ebook) | LCC LB1028.43 .S45 2019 (print) | DDC
   371.33--dc23
LC record available at https://lccn.loc.gov/2019001774

Typeset in 11 on 15 Adobe Garamond by
Servis Filmsetting Ltd, Stockport, Cheshire
Printed and bound in Great Britain by TJ International Limited

For further information on Polity, visit our website: politybooks.com

CONTENTS

The digital automation of teaching is set to be one of the defining educational challenges of the next twenty years. While the deployment of human-looking robots in classrooms remains more of a publicity stunt than a serious educational trend, many other forms of digital automation are being implemented across schools and universities around the world. Teachers are not being replaced by physical robots *per se*, but are increasingly surrounded by software, apps, platforms and other forms of artificial intelligence designed to carry out pedagogical tasks.

Most teachers remain confident that they are unlikely to be pushed aside by 'intelligent systems' any time soon. Nevertheless, teachers at all levels of education already face the prospect of working alongside these technologies. Thus, it is certainly worth exploring the extent to which human teachers might be displaced by machines in the near future. What aspects of teaching might it soon no longer make sense for humans to perform? Can automated systems free teachers up to work in different and more rewarding ways? Alternatively, will the humans who remain employed in education settings be compelled to work in an increasingly machine-like manner?

These are no longer frivolous or far-fetched questions. Powerful technologies are now being designed to autonomously support various types of learning – from infants picking up their first words through to physicians honing their surgical skills. A billion-dollar 'EdTech' market continues to grow as investors, developers and self-styled 'edu-preneurs' strive to overturn traditional modes of education, while also making tidy profits. The matter of how people learn (and, it follows, how people are supported in their learning) continues to be an area that is widely considered ready for innovation, reform and 'disruption'. The long-held professional status of school teachers and university lecturers is definitely under threat.

Amidst this hyperbole, it is important to remain level-headed and think carefully about the likely implications and broader consequences of such developments. There is little point in writing a book that simply celebrates the different forms of automated teaching that now exist. Instead these are technologies that need to be challenged and problematized. Yet critiquing the impending automation of education is no easy task, not least because discussions of the future are inherently speculative in nature. In many ways, then, this book is concerned ultimately with what we want from education in the near future – the values that we feel should be associated with children and young people's learning, the purposes that we want to ascribe to higher education, and the priorities that lie behind vocational training. These are definitely not straightforward technical issues. As such, our discussions need to engage with the politics of digital automation as much as with matters of design and efficiency.

These bigger-picture concerns are reflected in the choice of book title. The book might have been titled *Can Robots Replace Teachers?* However, it does not take long to see that the answer to this particular question is a resounding 'Yes'. As the next five chapters will detail, there are already plenty of devices, systems and applications that are capable of dealing with various aspects of teaching work. Another quickly answered alternative title would be *Will Robots Replace Teachers?* Again, in short, the answer to this question is 'Probably . . . if we let them'. There is already a growing appetite for specific forms of teaching work no longer being carried out by humans – for example, taking attendance registers and grading assignments. Instead, the most pertinent question to ask is *Should Robots Replace*

Teachers? Given that we are now starting to see the mainstream use of these powerful technologies, what do we want to happen?

Titling this book toward 'should' rather than 'could' moves the discussion into the realm of values, judgements and politics – reminding us that the integration of any technology into society should always be approached as a choice. The fact that automated teaching technologies are now being designed and developed does not mean that they will inevitably be used in consistent ways with predetermined outcomes. History shows that technological change is non-linear, contingent and influenced by the different social contexts in which it is implemented. The ways in which technology unfolds across societies are never fully predictable or knowable. This uncertainty is what makes the prospect of any new digital technology exciting (but also dangerous). As such, it is crucial that we consider the possibility of alternative technological pathways and different digital futures for education.

So, while the headline of robots 'taking over education' might seem a fanciful proposition, there are some serious issues that deserve our sustained consideration. The digital automation of teaching work is not simply a technical matter of how to most effectively design, program and implement systems. Instead, we need to get to grips with questions relating to the nature of education as a profoundly social – and therefore human – process. These are questions about the sociology and psychology of education, about relationships and emotions, about education politics and education cultures. As Judy Wajcman contends, it is important that non-technologists get involved in shaping conversations around AI and take a leading role in 'crafting the future . . . gaze fixed on the horizon, alert to the winds of change'.[1]

As with all discussions about technology and society, these are difficult questions with no easy answers. This is a book that explores the big issues behind what can often appear to be unfathomably sophisticated tools and techniques. Rather than telling readers exactly what to think, the main aim of this book is to expand the nature of conversations about the future of teaching in the digital age. As the chapters progress, various arguments emerge for slowing down and fighting back against the excessive automation of education. Yet these arguments simply reflect my personal take on the topic . . . ultimately no one can be completely certain of how things will unfold. So, it is important to not take everything that is argued in this book as an inevitable fact or irrefutable truth. However nuanced and informed they might be, all discussions about the future of technology involve large doses of speculative thinking and guess-work. We cannot be sure of exactly what *will* happen, but we should at least be clear about what we would *prefer* to happen. Get ready to make up your mind!

Many thanks to Sofia Serholt for helping me make sense of the issues around physical robots in the classroom. Thanks also to Selena Nemorin for her initial efforts to get me interested in issues around robots and AI. Thanks to Dragan Gašević and Carlo Perrotta for their conversations about computer science and the finer points of AI, machine learning and data science. Readers from the AIED community included two anonymous readers recruited by Polity Press – both of whom were very generous in providing helpful comments on a book that they clearly did not fully agree with. Thanks also to colleagues at the Monash Faculty of Education who have helped me get to grips with the issues around teachers and teaching. These include Paul Richardson and Jennifer Bleazby. I would also like to thank Mary Savigar and Ellen MacDonald-Kramer at Polity for initially pitching the title, and for their subsequent editorial support. Thanks also to Tim Clark for copy-editing the manuscript.

'This is a book that explores the big issues behind what can often appear to be unfathomably sophisticated tools and techniques.'

ONE

AI, Robotics and the Automation of Teaching

*If we teach today's students as we taught yesterday's, we
rob them of tomorrow*
John Dewey

THE ROBOTS ARE COMING! In fact, robots have
been coming for a long time now. Over the past
sixty years Robbie, HAL, R2-D2 and Wall-E have
been established as mainstays of popular culture, while
their 'real-life' equivalents regularly make headline
news. Many people still recall chess grandmaster Garry
Kasparov being defeated by IBM's Deep Blue in 1997,
while Hanson Robotics' 'Sophia' gained notoriety in
2016 as the first humanoid robot to be granted national
citizenship. Regardless of their context, people certainly
take notice of robots. There is something about these
machines that seems to provoke strong reactions and
soul-searching about what it means to be human.

Beyond being a regular feature of news reports
and science fiction, the primary practical significance
of robots relates to the changing nature of contemporary work. A wide range of jobs and professions

1

face the prospect of increased high-tech automation. Industries such as circuit-board manufacturing, underground mining, and fruit-picking are now reliant on automated, mechanized robots. Elsewhere, intelligent systems are expected to soon take the place of human doctors, lawyers and accountants. High-tech automation is seen as a genuine proposition across many sectors of work and employment.

A notable exception to this trend is education. Despite occasional speculation over 'computer tutors' and 'robot teachers', it has been generally assumed that education is one area of work destined to remain the preserve of humans. Most people intuitively feel that education is an essentially human undertaking. While disagreeing on many other points, education experts broadly concur that learning is a social process dependent on interactions with more knowledgeable others. All told, the belief persists that learning is something best guided by expert human teachers in socially rich settings.

Such thinking is certainly reinforced by the continued dominance of mass schooling and lecture-based university degrees. Yet the past two decades have seen significant technological advances in areas of artificial intelligence (AI) such as robotics and machine learning. These technologies are increasingly social in nature, and able to operate at speeds and scales that far outstrip the capacity of any human. This is beginning to fuel demands from outside the education sector to reconsider the 'cookie-cutter' model of a single teacher presiding over twenty students. Instead, it is claimed that AI technologies are now capable of supporting superior forms of education that do not entail the central involvement of a human teacher. Given this, we need to seriously consider the implications of robotics, artificial intelligence and the digital automation of teaching work.

Robots and artificial intelligence

We first need to establish some basic terms of reference. What concepts and ideas underpin the question of 'robots' replacing 'teachers'? In terms of the technological aspect of these discussions, it helps to move quickly on from imagining robots in the guise of R2-D2 or Wall-E. Of course, 'physical robots' *are* being used in education, and certainly raise a host of interesting issues (these will be tackled in Chapter 2). Yet robotics is just one area involving the application of artificial intelligence. In this sense, our interests lie primarily with the broad field of AI and associated advances in machine learning and big data.

The field of artificial intelligence emerged in the 1950s as computer scientists became interested in developing machines capable of thinking intelligently. Up until the 2010s, AI work focused mainly on the challenge of adding 'thinking-like' features to computerized technology. This involves a number of different ingredients to provide the computer with an expert knowledge base, codified reasoning and logics required to make decisions. One important aspect of this work is based around the concept of machine learning. This is the process of algorithms being 'trained' to parse large amounts of data in order to learn how to make informed decisions and perform tasks. Adrian Mackenzie describes this as using data to lend a degree of 'computability', predictability and control to real-life phenomena.[1] Until recently, these forms of machine learning tended to focus on relatively specific tasks, with any AI system requiring the guidance of programmers to steer it toward correct calibrations. However, the 2010s saw machine learning take on a more powerful guise – what is termed 'deep learning'.

There has been much recent excitement over deep learning as the key to developing forms of AI with the potential to radically transform areas of society such as education. One of the central characteristics of deep learning is the application of machine learning techniques to artificial neural networks. These are networks modelled on the complex layered structure of biological brains. Deep learning involves sets of training data being continually dis-assembled and re-assembled through the layers of an artificial neural network, with each network node continually assigning different weightings to a specific data point. Crucially, a deep learning system is able to train *itself* to refine the accuracy of these algorithms until they are capable of reaching accurate conclusions. This capacity to learn autonomously using the operating principles of neural networks is seen to offer the possibility of achieving powerful levels of 'human-like' reasoning and language skills – what some commentators see as 'the holy grail' of 'generalized intelligence'.[2]

An early 'proof of concept' for deep learning came from a team of Google engineers led by Andrew Ng in 2012, training huge neural networks on data from 10 million YouTube videos. This breakthrough took advantage of three technological developments of the time – the reduced cost of graphics processing units, the vast storage capacity of cloud computing, and the growing availability of massive data sets. In particular, the early 2010s marked a tipping point in 'big data', with terabytes of digital content being generated every hour through digital sensors, social media and other commonplace technologies. This massive volume of available data is seen to have transformed the potential of machine learning. As Andrew Ng has since reflected: 'The analogy to deep learning is that the rocket engine is the deep learning models and the fuel is the huge amounts of data we can feed to these algorithms.'[3]

These processes now underpin various types of AI application. For example, machine learning is a key element of the image processing capabilities that underpin the operation of self-driving tractors and autonomous drone weaponry. Elsewhere, big data processing is used to identify people and locations at increased risk of crime (so-called 'predictive policing'), and to configure forms of customized healthcare through the analysis of population-wide genomic data (so-called 'precision medicine'). Many of these advances are driven by the expansion of types of digitized data. For example, the emerging field of 'affective computing' seeks to detect and recognize human emotions from a range of data relating to facial detection, body gestures, galvanic skin response and other physiological measurements. To paraphrase a long-standing business mantra, there is now a growing belief that 'if you can't measure it, you can't improve it'.

Despite such enthusiasms, the fast-expanding scope of these applications is proving contentious. For every optimistic declaration of 'better living through AI' there are concerns over inaccuracies, misrecognitions and faulty decision-making. The growing hype around big data and machine learning has highlighted the fact that AI systems are only as good as the logics they are programmed with and the data sets they are trained on. While cases of computer vision processing failing to distinguish between sheep and grass are understandably embarrassing for the developers involved, failures of AI applications to recognize African-American faces as human are clearly discriminatory.[4] Automated image misrecognition can lead to a cat being mistaken for a dog, *or* an Afghani wedding party mistaken for a military convoy. Algorithmic sorting has already led to unjust decisions in criminal sentencing and social welfare payments.[5] AI has quickly become an area of computer science associated with profound social consequences.

Many AI developers and vendors acknowledge these shortcomings but see them as teething troubles that will eventually be overcome. These systems are designed to become more accurate and efficient with increased use over time. As a result, many proponents of AI reason that any short-term limitations should be seen in light of the potential for longer-term transformations on an unprecedented scale. Some commentators anticipate the development of 'a distributed planetary computer of enormous power'[6] involving billions of connected processors working with a continuous supply of data from millions of data sources. Others see the potential realization of the 'technological singularity' where artificial superintelligence suddenly begins to outstrip human intelligence and prompt a new evolutionary phase. It is generally hoped that such scenarios will be life-enhancing rather than life-threatening. As Garry Kasparov has argued in his latter-day role as an ambassador for 'responsible robotics': 'new forms of AI will surpass us in new and surprising ways . . . Humans, meanwhile, will continue up the ladder . . . We're not being replaced by AI. We're being promoted.'[7]

Teachers and teaching

Alongside the complexity of AI technologies, we also need to be mindful of the multi-layered nature of this book's other topic of discussion – the 'teacher'. Most discussions of AI and education spend surprisingly little time reflecting on the nature and form of teaching. Ten years of being taught at school seems to give many people strong but inevitably partial opinions on what teaching is and what teachers do. Yet, as will be stressed throughout this book, teaching is something that is as equally complicated as AI. If we are to properly do justice to this book's title, we need to unpack exactly what it is that teachers do.

In a basic sense, a teacher is anyone who supports others to learn – that is, helps them acquire knowledge and skills. As John Dewey reasoned, no one can claim to be teaching unless someone else is learning. Of course, learning is never completely abstract or content-free. A teacher therefore possesses some sort of expert knowledge about what is being learned. In addition, teachers also require knowledge and experience of 'pedagogy' – a broad term referring to strategies, skills, understandings and theories of how to teach. After all, many experts in a subject area turn out to be lousy teachers. In this sense, a teacher is anyone combining these two aspects of 'content knowledge' and 'pedagogical knowledge'.

There are many different roles that fit these basic criteria. Professors, lecturers, trainers, mentors and guides might all consider themselves to be 'teachers'. Within adult education – particularly in business and industry settings – teachers can also take the role of trainers, instructors and coaches. While teachers are usually responsible for groups and classes, others work with individual students in a tutoring capacity. Common to all these roles is the job of supporting the learning process within some form of organized setting or structure (whether a kindergarten or a corporate training centre). Regardless of the specific setting, a teacher will nearly always have undergone a period of specialist training and professional socialization. One cannot simply brand oneself a 'teacher' – this is a highly skilled and privileged role.

Given the importance accorded to education in every society, there has been much philosophizing over what a teacher should be. Many people still look back to Plato's description of the Socratic method where the teacher acts as a dialogic 'midwife', prompting dialectic questioning of alternative perspectives, and leading the learner to discover and refine understandings.[8] Of course, these high-minded ancient ideals often bear little resemblance to the roles and tasks that today's teachers find themselves undertaking. The practicalities of teaching usually involve detailed planning, organization and management of work. As with any leading role within an institution, teachers are also often responsible for regulatory and disciplinary functions, as well as considerable amounts of administration and bureaucracy. Ironically, school and university teachers frequently find their time taken up by requirements to produce evidence of their teaching, rather than opportunities to actually teach.

These realities of teaching work need to be remembered whenever we are presented with over-romanticized descriptions of teaching. Yet throughout our subsequent discussions, it will be important to retain a sense of what might be realistically considered as 'good' teaching. This is where experts in the fields of education and AI tend to diverge significantly. As we will see throughout this book, a privileged version of teaching amongst many technologists is the ideal of individual instruction in the guise of a one-to-one tutor. Technologists are fond of recalling the '2 Sigma' phenomenon reported by Benjamin Bloom, which reportedly found that students learning from one-to-one tutorials performed at considerably higher levels than those receiving conventional classroom instruction. Computer scientists wax lyrical about the Athenian philosopher-tutors and the children of Chinese emperors receiving bespoke classical tutoring. In contrast, most other forms of teaching tend to be presumed inferior. As Terry Sejnowski put it, 'few can afford individual instruction, and the assembly-line classroom system found in most schools today is a poor substitute'.[9]

Most education experts take a different view – seeing value in collective, institutionally provided learning. Acknowledging that it is fanciful to expect contemporary teachers to live up to the Socratic ideal, a fairly robust consensus has formed during the past 100 years over what makes for 'good' teaching. For example, it is now widely recognized that teaching (of any kind) is never simply a process of transferring knowledge and skills over to students – what might be characterized as 'the filling of empty vessels'. Instead, a good teacher will work hard to structure their students' learning and help individuals make connections with new knowledge. This might involve allowing learners to experiment, explore and discover things 'for themselves', but always with the underlying support and direction of the teacher.

This view of teaching reflects the view that teachers are part of what David Cohen terms the 'human improvement professions'.[10] This idea of 'human improvement' therefore broadens the focus of teaching to include the development of character as well as the acquisition of knowledge. Writing during the early twentieth century, the philosopher John Dewey saw teaching as cultivating the 'habit' of learning that is necessary for someone to thrive as a member of a democratic community. Eighty years later, most educators still aspire toward working in ways that address this wide-ranging brief. Teaching is therefore seen to involve supporting the development of a learner's head, heart and soul. This is intricate work to be taking on.

AI and teaching – big hopes and complex issues

These latter arguments from the likes of Dewey and Cohen highlight the complexity of teaching, and the grand ambitions of any human *or* machine that aspires toward being a teacher. This raises a straightforward question – if teaching is a 'human improvement profession' then are humans always in the best position to improve other humans? Clearly some people are not convinced that teaching should always be left to humans. Indeed, there are growing calls – especially from outside the education profession – for AI-driven technologies to work alongside (or even instead of) human teachers.

The hype surrounding AI and education is growing in support and substance. This is an area of fast-growing commercial interest, attracting the attention of 'Big Tech' giants such as IBM and Google, alongside specialist education developers such as Pearson and Metacog. It is estimated that the global market for AI in education will grow from $537 million in 2018 to $3,683 million by 2023.[11] At the same time, university researchers are also exploring possible AI applications in education – from engaging learners with autism through to the development of personalized learning companions.

These efforts coalesce in the field of 'AIED' research, which combines computer science, education, psychology and other facets of the learning sciences.

These activities are fuelling expectation and the hope of imminent change in the provision of education for learners of all ages. AI researchers have long considered themselves on the brink of being able to support vastly superior ways in which humans can engage with knowledge. As Terry Sejnowski puts it, 'as more and more cognitive appliances are devised . . . humans will become smarter and more capable in ways that we have not yet foreseen'.[12] Some researchers therefore feel emboldened to proclaim that 'AI will be a game changer in education.'[13] A few commentators have begun to put their necks on the line, proclaiming boldly that robots will replace teachers 'within the next ten years'.[14] Others predict more modestly that teachers can soon expect to have their own 'AI assistant'.[15] Either way, many commentators appear certain that classrooms and schools are unlikely to remain unaffected for much longer. As Donald Clark reasons: 'At some point we may look back at teachers and classrooms as we look back on manual manufacturing in factories. I'm not suggesting that teachers are in any way not valuable or smart, just that AI technology may, as in many other areas, get more valuable and smarter.'[16]

At first glance, these predictions make intuitive sense. After all, tremendous advances have been made in AI over the past ten years, and humans cannot expect to have a monopoly over every job. As Kristin Houser writes, 'it's easy to see the appeal of using a robotic teacher . . . Digital teachers wouldn't need days off and would never be late for work . . . the systems would never make mistakes. If programmed correctly, they also wouldn't show any biases toward students based on gender, race, socio-economic status, personality preference, or other consideration.'[17] Yet, when it comes to education, making a distinction between 'humans' and 'technology' is much more difficult than it might appear, highlighting a couple of salient points that we need to take with us throughout this book.

First, it is important to remind ourselves that not all 'humans' are the same, and certainly not all humans make good teachers. It is important not to blindly defend 'human' teachers as a noble breed that is above criticism. There are some people currently working as teachers who are obviously ill-suited to the job and fully merit being replaced immediately. There are also some aspects of teaching work that can undoubtedly be done better by machines. Most teachers' working days involve routine obligations and 'practical' tasks that do not involve engaging directly with learners and their learning. For example, it is reasonable to presume a robot or computer to be an adequate substitute for a teacher whose only job is to deliver chunks of information and keep records of attendance. Instead, the most important issues that this book needs to consider relate to the potential of AI technology to replicate the work of a *good* human teacher. A couple of important questions therefore run throughout the following chapters: (i) what does 'good' (rather than bad) teaching entail, and (ii) what elements of this might be suitable for technology-based provision?

Second, it is increasingly difficult to separate 'technology' from 'humans'. One of the key points that quickly emerges in any serious discussion of AI is that all technology is 'human' in its origins and implementation. Any 'robot teacher' is actually a combination of people and machines, the material world, coded structures and social settings. Thus, it is important to remember that robots are designed and configured by human designers, and that algorithms are scripted by human programmers. Similarly, most 'machine learning' actually involves computers trying to discern patterns from the aggregated actions of millions of humans. If we want to make sense of the use of AI technology in education we therefore need to take a 'socio-technical' approach – that is, see technology as a combination of technical and scientific factors, alongside economic, political, social and cultural issues. Distinguishing between 'human teachers' and 'robot teachers' is not a matter of people versus machines. Instead, we are concerned with how different sets of people are entwined with machines and software in increasingly complex and closely connected ways.

AI and education – seeing the bigger picture

This socio-technical perspective certainly pushes us to think about the wider connotations of AI-driven education. These are not advances that are arising solely from the intellectual curiosity of a few technologists, developers and researchers. Instead, enthusiasms for putting AI systems into classrooms correspond with broader political struggles over the future of education and the nature of the emerging 'digital age'. This includes some significant wider agendas that need to be kept in mind as our discussions progress.

Techno-solutionism and the increasing influence of Silicon Valley

First, efforts to introduce forms of AI into education are just one of many broad reforming activities of Big

Tech companies – reflecting a distinct Silicon Valley set of values that are an increasingly prominent component of global capitalism. Alongside an interest in everything from low-income healthcare through to high-speed public transportation, these influences are pushing for substantive shifts in how the improvement and reform of education is conceived. Such work involves a fundamental faith in what Evgeny Morozov has termed 'technological solutionism'[18] – i.e. the belief that digital technologies offer a ready 'problem-solving infrastructure' that is capable of tackling complex social problems. Such thinking underpins the assumption that problems in education can be addressed through applying AI-driven operational logics that have proven successful elsewhere (such as Uber and Netflix). Key here is a willingness to approach education change in an 'entrepreneurial' fashion – experimenting with substantially funded educational interventions that can be rapidly modified and terminated if not proven successful. This approach is celebrated as embodying a 'fail fast, fail often' mentality of software development, with an emphasis on 'beta-testing' possible solutions that might later be scaled-up on a system-wide basis.

Corporate desires to reform education

In addition, current support for AI-driven education chimes with a wider belief that schools and universities will benefit from high-tech innovation and 'digital disruption'. This itself feeds into the growing corporate impatience to reform what are perceived as outdated and inefficient education systems. Indeed, an increasingly prominent argument within the hyperbole that surrounds AI in education is the notion that current forms of school and university are 'broken', out of date and rapidly becoming not 'fit for purpose'. As a result, IT corporations, philanthropic foundations, venture capitalists and other 'edu-preneurs' are investing substantial amounts of time, finance and publicity in attempts to 'fix' and/or 'disrupt' traditional ideas of what a school or university is. Calls for the automation of classroom teaching are often driven by desires to 'reboot' twentieth-century education systems that many business interests suspect are relics from the industrial era.[19]

Political desires to reform/replace the teaching profession

Alongside these broader agendas, the idea of deploying AI in education chimes with growing political and popular disgruntlement with the teaching profession. The days of school teachers and university lecturers being highly respected members of the community have long gone. We are repeatedly told of a 'crisis' in teaching, with burnt-out teachers flocking to leave a profession which is further weakened by the declining quality of incoming recruits. Teaching and lecturing are demeaned as costly and over-unionized professions that are stubbornly resistant to change. Against this background, there is growing interest in alternative sources of teaching labour – such as schemes to fast-track unqualified graduates, business and military personnel into schools. The idea of deploying AI-driven teaching technologies clearly aligns with these ambitions to disrupt educational labour politics.

The future of work and end of the professions

Clearly, these discussions are also entwined with general concerns over the impact of AI on future forms of work. It is widely expected that AI will lead to the demise of many jobs and professions, while also necessitating the creation of other new forms of employment. Such concerns are accompanied by general talk of a digitally driven 'end of the professions'.[20] Professionals who rely on any sort of routine, structure or protocol are seen to be susceptible, including doctors, architects, therapists and even the clergy. In contrast to the usual concerns and hand-wringing over job losses, these shifts are often argued to be a progressive step – democratizing expertise away from the confines of professional elites, and reducing reliance on gatekeepers of expert advice and services. With the need for human journalists, accountants and lawyers in times of digital automation now being seriously questioned, it is perhaps unsurprising that the teaching profession is also coming under similar scrutiny.

The need to be critical

All these different issues and agendas imply that the topic of AI and education needs to be approached in a broad, balanced manner. The question *Should Robots Replace Teachers?* is not simply a technical matter of how to design and develop effective systems. Neither is it solely an educational issue of learning theory or pedagogical design. Instead, these are questions of society, history and humanity. The implementation of AI technologies in education should be seen as a complex and highly controversial matter. Indeed, we should not be content to accept the consequences of AI in education in an unquestioning, submissive manner. We need to avoid what Harry Collins terms the 'surrender' to what are clearly limited and in many ways unintelligent machines.[21] This book can (and will) do better than that!

As such, the rise of AI in education needs to be approached along social, cultural, economic and political lines. There are a number of important connections that need to be explored. Take, for instance, the ways in which technological change is entwined with a general shift in neoliberal societies toward the increased role of the private sector, increased individualism and a focus on data-driven efficiencies and accountabilities. As will be illustrated throughout this book, computational technologies chime with the ways in which contemporary educational institutions are now run along data-driven lines of numeric measurement and accountability.

Such sociological concerns also raise questions over possible inequalities associated with the increased automation of teaching. This relates to which groups of education workers are most likely to have their jobs compromised, as well as the varying standards of learning experienced by different social groups. It is unlikely that teachers and students in a private fee-paying school such as Eton will experience the same sort of automated schooling as a neighbouring government school. AI will impact on an Ivy League university such as Harvard in very different ways to a community college in Hudson County. In all these ways, then, we need to remain mindful of the politics of technology, and keep 'some critical distance on Silicon Valley's futurist discourse'.[22]

Any critical awareness of developments in AI and education is certainly strengthened by taking an interest in the histories of these 'new' technologies. The educational application of artificial intelligence stems back to the 1960s, with a crop of 'computer tutors' and similar systems being developed from that time onward. As such, the current wave of AIED innovations is not the first time that attempts have been made to automate teaching. As we shall see in later chapters, there are even clear parallels between the teaching technologies of the 2020s and the mechanized 'teaching machines' of the 1920s. While early twentieth-century machines usually relied on punch-hole cards, cogs and levers, some of the lessons learned from these past attempts at educational automation hold true for today – not least the complex and often contradictory implications of these technologies for educational institutions, teachers and students.

Finally, it is also important to acknowledge how AI in education is related closely to one of the primary existential challenges of our modern era – what does it mean to be human in a digital age? On the one hand, this raises a range of biological questions concerning the living organism of the human body, and the possible altered nature of teaching and learning with (and through) these bodies. But it also raises a number of questions regarding the changing emphasis on what it means to be an 'individual' in an increasingly connected world. For example, what does 'collective' existence mean as local, face-to-face obligations shift toward global, remote ways of being?

Yet perhaps the most important philosophical questions raised by AI in education concern moral and ethical debates over what we think is acceptable and/ or desirable. For example, should we always place the judgements of humans over those of machines? Should we always place the well-being of humans above machines – if so, does this extend to safeguarding the jobs of human teachers? Alternatively, if a technological system is proven to produce consistently better outcomes for learners than being taught by a human, then what grounds are there for refusing to use it? Should systems and applications that are proven to be effective in terms of learning outcomes (or perhaps simply of cost savings) be made obligatory? Or should we judge the technologies we use in terms of aspects of education relating to character-building, human improvement and the greater good? Indeed, what does the notion of 'the good life' and pursuing meaningful and humane forms of education now mean in an age of digital technologies and AI?

Conclusions

Having established these basic definitions and ground rules, we now need to get to the task in hand. What does the continued rise of AI mean for education? Many people might still consider these technologies a novelty as we enter the 2020s, but what might the consequences of AI be in a decade or so? These are important issues to start thinking about as quickly as possible. Indeed, it is worrying that the growing presence of AI in classrooms is not already provoking greater consternation and debate throughout education. Despite the obvious advantages to be gained from preparing for an increasingly automated future, education continues to be one of the *least* future-focused sectors there is. If anything, educators tend to take perverse professional pride in their capacity to deal with crises as they occur. Yet when it comes to AI and automation, resignedly waiting for the worst is likely to have ruinous results.

Up until now, agendas around AI and education have been dominated largely by computer scientists, cognitive psychologists, technology designers and vendors, business interests and corporate reformers. To what extent have these non-education concerns got it right? Alternatively, what does education have to offer in refining (or refuting) the claims currently being made by proponents of AI and education? An important thought to keep in mind throughout the next four chapters is the need to think otherwise. On the one hand, what can we learn about future reforms of education from the AI-based technologies that are already being developed? Alternatively, what issues arise that necessitate a rethinking of this technology and how it is implemented in education settings?

TWO

Physical Robots in the Classroom

Given this book's title, it seems fitting to start with the use of 'physical' robots in education. While few of these machines are being used regularly in educational settings, the development of physical robots for use in classrooms over the past twenty years raises some crucial issues that relate to all attempts at technologically replicating the work of human teachers. Chapters 3 and 4 will focus on AI-driven software systems and applications that are being used by millions of learners. In contrast, the technologies covered in this chapter are more likely to be used only by a few thousand students mainly in experimental contexts. Nevertheless, physical robots offer a neat opening test-case for this book to consider.

In contrast to their limited actual use in education settings, there is a rich history of speculation about physical robot teachers. Often this speculation has reflected broader societal concerns of the time. For example, media interest in robot teachers first peaked in the 1950s and 1960s as concerns grew in post-war countries over how to educate the fast-expanding 'baby boom' generation of children. Comic strips and TV series of the time featured robot teachers such as Superman's 'Super-Teacher from Krypton' and the Jetsons' 'Miss Brainmocker'. As the twentieth century drew to a close, some of these depictions took on more dystopian tones. The 1990 film *Class of 1999* depicted ex-military robots reassigned as teachers, with a tagline of 'Hired to Teach, Programmed to Kill'. In contrast, the actual implementation of classroom robots into the twenty-first century has proven far more perfunctory. So, what does the actual development of these machines in classrooms really look like? Most importantly, what does this tell us about AI and education?

Robots in the classroom

The most prevalent use of physical robots in classrooms to date is as a simple learning tool. Basic robotics has become a feature of high-school and undergraduate subjects, where students learn from building and programming robots to perform specific tasks. It is now commonplace to see robotics kits being assembled to explore the physics of kicking a ball or to learn basic engineering concepts. Unlike many comparable forms of education software, such hardware-oriented learning is seen as a powerful way to 'provide a tangible and physical representation of learning outcomes'.[1]

In contrast, this chapter is concerned with the far more sophisticated development of 'social' robots to act as teachers and classroom companions. This involves physical robots that can engage with learners as a social being – possessing some degree of autonomy and interacting in similar ways to a human teacher, peer or perhaps a domestic animal. Social robots are able to 'sense' their environment, plan how to achieve task-specific goals based on this knowledge, and then carry out these actions without external control.[2]

In reality, the teaching robots developed over the past twenty years vary from machines that have fully autonomous AI-driven capabilities to less sophisticated tele-presence devices that are partially controlled by remote human tutors. As such, a range of robots have been developed for educational use – all differing in terms of their ascribed role, the activities they engage in, and their appearance. For example, robots can be assigned to the roles of didactic tutor, classroom manager, student peer or less capable companion. All of these roles can involve different activities, from lecturing and testing, through to requiring guidance and teaching from humans. Finally, in terms of appearance, these machines can take a number of different guises – from stereotypical machine-like units, through humanoid mannequins and non-human characters (such as animals). Each of these is worth considering in a little more detail.

'Classroom teacher' robots

'Classroom teacher' robots are usually designed to act in the dual role of authority figure and as an explicit source of knowledge. Many of these machines take on rather stereotypical 'robot' forms of appearance in the form of relatively large wheeled units with arms, a head and some form of face. Research and development into autonomous interactive robots has been led by roboticists in Japan, Taiwan and South Korea, with their most popular use being as teacher substitutes in primary and middle-school settings. While these robots are sometimes styled as care-giving, they tend to be tasked with delivering direct instruction, maintaining class control and engaging students in learning activities.

Early efforts such as the IROBI robotic teaching assistants were relatively rudimentary, little more than mobile units with monitors in their midriff that students could interact with. Recent efforts have become more socially sophisticated, striving, as Sofia Serholt describes it, to 'emulate the conduct of charismatic teachers'.[3] Particular emphasis is now placed on these machines' ability to recognize and respond to learners' emotional and affective states. For example, using sensors and depth cameras, one recently developed classroom robot was proven able to track students' behaviour 95 per cent of the time, with a 66 per cent chance of correctly identifying each student. Significantly, the developers claim this data allowed their robot to calculate each student's 'social status' within their peer group 'with 71.4% accuracy'.[4] This information is intended to direct the robot's attention toward isolated or bullied children.

Alongside these uses as pre-school and primary-school tutors, another popular area for tutor robots is English language learning. This has spawned a specialized field of research in Robot Assisted Language Learning, focused largely on replicating the experience of direct one-on-one interaction with a native speaker.[5] Developers report that language learners are less hesitant to converse with robot tutors than with humans. Robots are certainly perceived as less judgemental about language errors and mistakes, ready to engage in repetitive instruction, while also able to provide visual cues, facial gestures and other non-verbal interactions that are considered to be important aspects of language learning.[6]

Humanoid robot teachers

While often physically designed to take on human-like dimensions, the robots just outlined are not intended to appear 'human' *per se*. Developers have tended to concentrate on ensuring these machines can operate autonomously without the need for human input. In contrast, only a few roboticists have attempted to test the effectiveness of humanoid teacher robots. These efforts have tended to be highly realistic in appearance but rather less autonomous in their actions.

One of the most publicized of these humanoid machines was the Japanese robot Saya. In a series of trials toward the end of the 2000s, Saya was presented to classes as a teacher, although actually largely controlled using so-called 'Wizard-of-Oz techniques'.[7] Saya took the guise of a female teacher, with fully prosthetic rubberized face and hands, skirt suit, brown hair and make-up. Saya was primarily an expressive 'face robot' mounted on a less malleable mannequin. The head had nineteen control points allowing manipulation of the neck, chin, nose, eyebrows, eyelids, jaw, chin and wrinkles. A series of motors allowed Saya's face to be programmed to express six basic emotions of happiness, sadness, surprise, fear, disgust and anger.

Saya was trialled successfully with eleven-year-old students, taking class registers, monitoring students' behaviour, delivering lectures while looking around the room. When in 'interaction mode' the robot could issue short sentences such as 'Do your best!', 'Be quiet!' and 'Don't look away'. The developers considered these exploratory studies to demonstrate that Saya was able to 'give people a feeling of human-like presence as if people were interacting with a real human'.[8] Tellingly, the robot seemed most successful in evoking active participation with elementary students in comparison to university students. As the chief scientist behind the Saya robot recounted, younger children 'even start crying when they are scolded'.[9]

Companion and peer robots

Tutor robots continue to be implemented in classrooms, largely as a 'proof of concept' that such technologies will be accepted by learners. In contrast, a small but enthusiastic number of roboticists have begun to explore the use of 'companion' robots in kindergartens and schools – usually making use of off-the-shelf models marketed to domestic consumers for as little as a few thousand dollars. Instead of being presented as authoritative figures, these robots are placed in educational settings to help students learn on an informal, playful basis. Some of these robots are programmed to take a novice and teachable role, with students learning from assisting the robot to 'learn' different tasks and procedures for itself.

These experiments have often involved the use of small moveable biped robots such as the Pepper and Nao units. While a few of these robots have been designed to appear as miniature humans (such as the Kaspar 'child' companion robot), there is also growing interest in the use of smaller table-top devices. A table-top robot such as Sota is only 24 centimetres tall, has no legs as such, and is able to connect to the internet and sensor-enabled devices. While less striking than their fully mobile walking counterparts, such robots have been trialled successfully in classrooms in a 'teaching peer' role. Sota can hold the attention of students, detect student identities at beginning of class, discern silences to enable turn-taking, and simulate approval or disapproval by changing eye colour.[10] While not able to roam around the classroom, these forms of robot have proven to be surprisingly engaging and educative.

One of the key goals when developing classroom-based robot companions is the capacity for the machine to establish social bonds with the learner and offer a genuinely sociable presence.[11] As Takayuki Kanda and colleagues put it, roboticists are keen to tackle the 'social challenge' of designing machines 'to have something in common with their users'.[12] One common technique with younger children is to encourage physical contact between the learner and machine, such as patting, hugging and kissing the robot.[13] Other techniques include ensuring that robots can address students by name, become friendly over time and confide 'personal matters'. For example, after 540 minutes of contact time, Kanda's 'Robovie' unit is programmed to disclose its support for the Hanshin Tigers baseball team.

Care-eliciting robots

In contrast to these companion and peer style robots is the use of smaller machines designed to fulfil what is often described as 'care-eliciting' roles. The roboticist Fumihide Tanaka recounts first realizing the potential of these robots while trialling a companion robot programmed to dance and entertain a room of pre-schoolers. During one session this machine lost power and initiated a shut-down process where it slowly lay on its back. After some consternation, the children began to fetch blankets, food and generally care for the stricken robot. This prompted Fumihide to explore the educative value of what he terms 'defective' and 'not-so-smart' robots in eliciting help and stimulating student cooperation. As he describes it, these are 'robots designed to arouse in humans a wide range of caring behaviors'.[14]

Fumihide has successfully used this approach with the popular Pepper robot. Other researchers have explored the educational use of the Paro robot baby seal, seeking to replicate the success of this machine with elderly dementia patients. Paro responds to being touched and petted, and is programmed to seek out eye contact and remember familiar faces. Beneath its touch-sensitive fur, whiskers and big glassy eyes, Paro is equipped with 32-bit processors, microphones, tactile sensors and an intricate system of motors and actuators that move its body. Paro is reported to be an especially effective tool for children with autism, who also respond well to similar robotic dogs, dolls and teddy bears.[15] In contrast to replicating the presence of an authoritarian teacher at the front of the class, these machines are seen to support therapeutic learning in ways that human educators might struggle to achieve.

The potential and practicalities of classroom robots

Proponents of educational robotics certainly consider themselves to be making substantial progress. Despite most of these machines being in preliminary states of development, this is an area of considerable enthusiasm and anticipation. Take the following conclusion from a recent research project:

> In the future, the teacher's job could be performed more effectively by robots. The ability of machines to process huge amounts of information, and utilize the output for addressing student needs, underscores [a] significant area where AI surpasses humans. The same applies to the ability to interact with human learners without human emotions getting in the way. Maintaining a team of satisfied teachers is challenging, but if they are robots, it can be done much less expensively through AI, indicating that robots could be good substitutes for human teachers.[16]

In particular, many roboticists feel their work demonstrates a growing trust and acceptance of robots in teaching roles. For example, European studies have found over three-quarters of students to be positive about the idea of robots in the classroom, although not necessarily favouring complete replacement of their teachers.[17] Of course, the widespread integration of any type of physical robot in classrooms faces a number of practical barriers. These include the basic logistical challenges of keeping robots accommodated, powered and maintained in working order. Many school and university infrastructures struggle to maintain a collection of laptop computers, let alone a fleet of mechanically sophisticated robots. These machines remain prone to over-heating and malfunctioning. Similarly, teachers point to a lack of training and preparedness for sharing classrooms with such machines.[18]

These issues all replicate long-standing barriers to the implementation of any 'new' technology in education. Larry Cuban's history of 'pre-digital' technology use identified similar sets of barriers impeding the take-up of film, radio and television between the 1910s and 1980s.[19] While roboticists argue that these mitigating issues are likely to recede as robots become integrated throughout society, it might be harder to alter the suspicion that physical robot teachers are simply not good enough at the job of teaching. Experts acknowledge that most of the employment advantages prompting the implementation of robots in other industries do not apply to robot teachers.[20] Teaching is not an especially dangerous, dirty or dull task. Physical robots are not particularly cost-effective and, significantly, 'there is no compelling evidence that robots are better than humans at teaching'.[21] As such, developers mainly expect small pockets of demand from educators over the next decade or so to be for companion robots and language tutor robots. There is little prospect of millions of next generation Saya or Sota units taking over classrooms any time soon.

However, these limitations should not lead us to discount the *idea* of robot teachers altogether. Those roboticists pursuing work in this area clearly believe that they are capable of developing technologies that at some point can match human teachers. There is no reason to presume that robots will *never* become a viable educational proposition. Furthermore, even if their actual adoption remains limited, the concept of the physical teaching robot raises a number of important issues regarding the general implementation of AI in education. So, despite these current practical limitations, what broader issues does the idea of robot teachers bring to our attention?

How it 'feels' to be taught by a non-human

The development of classroom robots certainly raises interesting questions about the experience of being in the presence of these machines (and not being in the presence of a human teacher). What sort of relationships can humans have with (and through) machines? What does it mean for a teacher to be physically present? What role does body language, gesture and other tacit communication play in learning? Clearly, there are some tangible physiological and psychological differences when interacting with a 'teacher' robot which is functioning in what might ordinarily be a human role.

These questions raise some complex issues. Take, for example, the differences between robot and human bodies. Despite the best efforts of the design teams behind Saya, Pepper and Kaspar, a physical robot does not look, feel, speak or move as a human would. While not intended to look exactly like humans, nearly all of the robots outlined in this chapter approximate the physical presence of a child or large pet. These machines therefore draw attention to what it is like to be taught in the absence of a human body. Of course, human bodies are sidelined in many forms of technology-based education (in particular, online learning), yet the lack of a human body is particularly noticeable in situations where physical machinery is presented as a bodily substitute.

In this sense, physical robots remind us that the body is what Marcel Mauss described as a human's 'first and most natural instrument'.[22] Regardless of how nimble and dexterous they are, physical robots are only able to clumsily replicate how human teachers can use their bodies when teaching. Much teaching takes place through movement, for example turning to face the class or pacing around a room. There are various ways in which teachers utilize an 'expressive body' – i.e. raising or lowering their voice, raising an eyebrow, directing their gaze, choosing to dress in a particular manner. These actions all illustrate how human bodies are a valuable means of deploying 'intentional, projective power' in a classroom[23] – orchestrating the timing and rhythm of events, focusing attention, and generally 'setting the scene' for learning. The human body is not simply a supplementary element of a teacher's practice. Instead, the body energizes and anchors the whole performance of teaching.

It is therefore interesting to reflect on the limited ways in which robot teachers can use their bodies to teach. Saya was pre-programmed with different facial expressions, while Sota's eyes can change colour. Yet however sophisticated these simulations might be, issues of physical appearance are a recurring limitation of being taught by any of these machines. Human learners will respond to the fleshy biological body of another human in a way that is different to even the most realistic-looking simulation. Meeting the gaze of another person is qualitatively different than looking into the 'eyes' of a 3D humanoid robot, let alone a 24-centimetre table-top torso or an animatronic seal.

One common stumbling block to robotics research is how discomforting these robots can 'feel' to the humans they interact with, especially humanoid machines intended to resemble real people. Some of the field trials described earlier have reported younger children beginning to physically abuse the machines after the initial novelty subsides – hitting, pushing and generally disrespecting their robot teachers. While this may partially be due to a perceived lack of consequences, there is certainly something unsettling about being in the presence of these machines. Despite huge technical advances, many people continue to respond unfavourably to the 'creepy' appearance of lifelike prosthetic skin and pre-programmed facial emotions.

Other trials have shown how children's interactions with robot tutors can break down due to the robots' unhuman-like behaviour – for example, in terms of their discretion and fairness, as well as their not being able to identify areas of misunderstanding that a human could quickly gloss over and move on from.[24] Students will understandably react unfavourably to any teacher who is obsessively pedantic and indiscriminately puni-tive. In addition, roboticists still struggle to overcome the phenomenon of the 'Uncanny Valley' – i.e. the tendency of even the most lifelike simulation of a human to remain not *quite* realistic enough to dispel an unnerving, otherworldly sense. No teacher (however robotic) wants their appearance to send young children into floods of tears.

The ethics of robot teachers

Despite this potential creepiness, the most important questions about classroom robots undoubtedly concern the software, systems and virtual automation behind the physical 'skin'. Regardless of their aesthetics, it is important to remember that these physical robots are interfaces for incredibly complex software and AI-driven models of teaching and learning. In short, the issue is not how Saya or Sota look but what these machines are programmed to do. The most recent generations of classroom robots are computational systems designed to learn for themselves, develop logic processes and formulate mental models in order to make complex decisions. In this sense, the idea of intelligent systems making decisions and then acting on them clearly has ethical implications. The question here is deceptively simple: what moral principles should govern what we do with robots in education, and what should we configure robots to do 'of their own accord'?

Guidance can be found in the growing field of robo-ethics that has developed to make sense of the ethical implications and consequences of autonomous robots. These discussions understandably gravitate toward the application of automated technologies in medicine and military contexts – for example, the implications of developing what are dispassionately termed 'lethal autonomous weapons systems'. Yet concerns over ethics apply equally to the use of automated technologies in education. In fact, questions over what constitutes 'harm' in an educational context are less clear-cut than on a battlefield.

Many debates in robo-ethics are concerned with life-or-death concerns over what is intended to be achieved with AI – for example, whether it is acceptable to decide to 'precision' bomb a civilian target or turn off a life-support machine. In terms of education, then, few people would have similar qualms about the general implications of AI-based systems that are designed to support learners to learn. Nevertheless, a number of more specific ethical issues can be raised about the ways in which technologies are used to achieve this goal of 'supporting' learning. As such, the ethics of teaching robots relate to more nuanced questions regarding how a system or application carries out a specific task.

For example, the implementation of physical robots in education raises clear issues of privacy in terms of the data being gathered. Many of the robots described in this chapter rely on sensors, video monitoring or other forms of data gathered to help the machine 'sense' the learners it is working with. If a robot is silently calculating a learner's 'social status' does the individual have a right to be made aware of that fact, or perhaps be informed what is then being done with the data? Concerns can also be raised over the potential for these technologies to exacerbate inequalities between different groups of students. How will the benefits of advanced decision-making systems be distributed evenly? How can we ensure that the actions and decisions of these machines are not discriminatory?

Another set of important ethical issues relates to how students engage with and come to trust robots. Most of the technologies outlined in this chapter are designed to form emotional bonds with humans. Engineers working in the field of Human Robot Interaction deliberately focus on designing characteristics such as anthropomorphism, animacy, likeability, perceived intelligence and perceived safety.[25] To what extent are these features (especially in relation to young children) emotionally manipulative and deceptive?[26] Should we allow children to form emotional attachments with machines that they mistakenly perceive as cognitively sentient? Alternatively, is contact with a machine-based tutor a diminished, second-rate experience? Sherry Turkle has long warned against the risks of robots depriving learners of human contact – providing an 'illusion' of human relationships without all of the rich, messy and demanding aspects.[27] The possible 'harms' of learning alongside these machines are clearly subtle and not immediately obvious.

The politics of robot teachers

One usually unvoiced question lying behind the educational application of physical robots is why these particular technologies are believed to be a good idea. Many readers might well find the technologies described in this chapter as somewhat bizarre or outlandish. This raises the question of why such a reaction might *not* be similarly provoked by the software-based technologies which will be outlined in Chapters 3 and 4. In this sense, the development of classroom robots draws attention to the importance of context in shaping the take-up of any new technology. It is telling that the development of autonomous classroom robots has traditionally tended to be led by East Asian (particularly Japanese) researchers and developers. Why has enthusiasm for social robotic 'teachers' not been as enthusiastically pursued in other parts of the world? And what can this tell us about the likely spread of other AI technologies in education?

A number of social, economic, political and cultural issues can be seen to underpin the 'robotic turn' within Japanese society. Firstly, from a global economic perspective, there has been a concerted strategic focus within Japanese industry and government on robotics as the next 'new' technology, with a view to re-establishing the country as a world-leading high-tech economy and 'robot superpower'. While the worldwide market for industrial robots has stabilized, Japanese policymakers have identified the use of social robots in daily life as a likely next boom area for robot manufacturing. This has led to ambitious target-setting and funding for robotics in healthcare, social welfare and public service.

Yet the Japanese enthusiasm for robot teachers stems far beyond economic competitiveness. Perhaps most significantly, Japanese society is beset by a combination of demographic problems – not least a rising shortage of labour, a rapidly ageing population and a declining birth-rate amongst younger women. These trends are compounded by a lingering resistance to becoming dependent on non-Japanese immigrant workers. Against this background, the introduction of robot workers into traditionally feminized professions (such as teaching, nursing, receptionist work) offers a potentially quick technical fix. Alongside issues of gender politics and ethnocentrism, it has also been reasoned that Japan is more subtly attuned to the idea of physical robots than many other cultures. For example, Japanese popular culture has long promoted positive narratives about robots, not least in popular forms of manga and anime. It is even suggested that dominant Japanese belief systems such as Shinto contain a number of complex animistic beliefs about the presence of vital energies and forces being present in all aspects of the world, including non-animate and non-living objects. It is certainly understandable that the idea of robot teachers might have different cultural, social and economic connotations in Tokyo than in Toronto.

Of course, we must be careful not to presume a uniquely 'natural' Japanese affinity with robots. Despite all the factors just outlined, robots are not rife throughout Japanese everyday life, and the best-selling consumer robots to date are US-manufactured room-cleaning Roombas. Similarly, techno-animistic beliefs are prominent in specific groups around the world, not least among Western computer scientists and AI researchers.[28] Nevertheless, the interest in social robots is certainly distinct in Japan and illustrates the need to make sense of educational AI in terms of local contexts rather than global imperatives.

It is therefore worth remembering that the social robot teacher is not simply a value-free tool or a 'piece of cool kit' that is likely to spread in popularity the world over. Any particular instance of AI technology is the result of specific cultural, social, economic and political conditions, and is not necessarily going to be taken up in the same ways in other contexts. As will be discussed later, some of the other 'personalized' teaching platforms reviewed in Chapters 3 and 4 might be seen to reflect particularly North American (even Californian) assumptions about individual liberties and freedom of choice. These technologies might understandably come across as impractical or unsettling to someone not influenced by US culture, politics and economics. As such, it is worth bearing in mind that any AI technology will come laden with implicit politics, and often entwined with particular agendas, aims and aspirations that may not translate smoothly across to other contexts.

Conclusions

While many roboticists see the development of robot teachers primarily in terms of establishing proof of concept, this particular application of AI throws up some interesting but complex issues that should be taken forward into the rest of our discussions. Of course, it is sensible to not completely dismiss the possible future adoption of classroom robots on a large-scale basis. While this continues to be a niche, research-based concern there are signs that specific forms of physical robotic presence in classrooms might be a growing possibility. For instance, the popularity of hardware-based companions such as Amazon's Alexa and the Google Home device might suggest that machines such as these are more realistic prospects than full-sized humanoids such as Saya. Similarly, table-top assistants such as Sota represent less intrusive robotic presences in everyday contexts. Such developments in consumer robotics suggest that it is worth keeping half an eye on future developments of physical robot teachers.

For the time being, however, we need to shift our attention toward more familiar forms of software-based 'teachers'. While there is something compelling about imagining school systems full of Saya and Sota units, physical robotics should not distract us from the multitude of other AI-driven teaching systems that are already embedded in millions of classrooms around the world. It is far more realistic to expect *software* robots to be controlling what goes on in the classrooms of the 2020s. These are coded systems that might not look, feel or smell like 'robots', yet are already at the forefront of the digital automation of teaching work. So, while we should not forget developments in physical robotics, we now need to explore the soft automation of teachers and teaching – more specifically, the software automation of what many technologists distinguish as tutors and tutoring.

THREE

Intelligent Tutoring and Pedagogical Assistants

For the time being, few people are coming into every-day contact with physical robots. However, many of us *are* becoming familiar with virtual assistants, artificial agents and other forms of software 'bots'. Personal computer users in the 1990s and 2000s might remember the animated Clippy paperclip that sporadically popped up to assist users in navigating Microsoft Office software. Similar agents now guide us through various online interactions – from grocery shopping to completing tax returns. Millions of people also interact frequently with Siri, Alexa and other speech-based assistants. These programmed representations of knowledgeable others are designed specifically to help people achieve things. So, if software can help us choose a holiday or write a letter, why should it not also help us to learn?

This chapter considers the educational implication of intelligent tutors and pedagogical agents. In simple terms, intelligent tutoring systems are sophisticated software packages that guide students along pre-modelled learning pathways. These systems are often coupled with programmed pedagogical agents to allow learners to interact with 'on-screen characters that facilitate instruction'.[1] Much early work in this field derived from computer animation, developing animated characters that acted as interfaces between learners and online learning content. Subsequent interest grew in the production of 'virtual human' teachers 'designed to look and behave like real people'.[2] These agents are variously configured to explain, demonstrate and test knowledge, as well as sometimes reassure, motivate or deliberately confuse learners. Some agents are programmed with distinct 'teacher' or 'tutor' personas while others are designed to take less direct educational approaches. All told, millions of young people and adults around the world now come into contact with such agents.

The rise of the 'intelligent tutor'

Interest in pedagogical agents stems from the emergence of computer-aided instruction (CAI) during the 1960s. This relates to long-held ambitions within the field of AI to develop intelligent software that a human would not be able to distinguish as machine-based (the so-called 'Turing Test'). In this manner, early educational developers were understandably inspired by ideas of AI, and interested in the potential of dialogic 'computer tutors'. Despite the rudimentary computer technology of the time (which was not based on AI *per se*), computer scientists considered themselves capable of eventually providing learning experiences comparable to that described by the ancient Greek philosophers. As Patrick Suppes argued:

> We should have by the year 2020, or shortly thereafter, computer-assisted instruction courses that have the features that Socrates thought desirable so long ago. What is said in Plato's dialogue Phaedrus about teaching should be true in the twenty-first century, but now the intimate dialogue between student and tutor will be conducted with a sophisticated computer tutor.[3]

Enthusiasm for computer tutors continued throughout the 1960s and 1970s. By the beginning of the 1970s a range of tutorial and coaching software systems had been developed around the principle of presenting material to learners and then asking questions. These systems worked on the basis of a programmed 'tutor' component that could monitor interactions between the learner and the system, and subsequently decide how and when to intervene. The steady improvement of AI capabilities throughout the 1970s saw the emergence of 'intelligent CAI'. One key technology here was Intelligent Tutoring Systems – envisaged as expert systems capable of providing sustained computer-based tutoring. Work on intelligent tutoring systems was grounded in developments in cognitive science, particularly cognitivist theories of learning. Cognitivist principles underpinned the idea of a computer-based intelligent system hosting a series of teaching exchanges with an individual. The intelligent system is designed to respond to a model of what the individual should ideally be doing during the task (known as the 'domain' or 'expert knowledge' model). The individual's actual performance is compared with this expert model and the system then troubleshoots where the learner's mental actions have deviated. On the basis of these comparisons, the system can then provide intelligent feedback to guide the individual in further attempts at similar tasks (the so-called 'tutor model').

The design of many contemporary intelligent tutoring systems continues to follow similar forms of 'coached problem-solving'.[4] These systems now offer considerable flexibility in the order in which actions can be performed. For example, many systems are based around a mastery approach, with individuals allowed to progress after mastering the majority of a given task. In contrast to 'dumb' forms of CAI (such as the drill-and-practice software prevalent in schools during the 1980s), intelligent tutoring systems have always been intended to help people learn by 'doing' rather than through instruction. In this way, such systems are considered to provide reliable and engaging forms of personal tutoring. If not wholly comparable to Socrates, these software tutors are certainly seen to be as good as the teaching that most people are likely to experience in their lifetime.

The first wave of pedagogical agents

Computer graphics, sound and sensing capabilities advanced considerably during the 1990s. As a result, tutoring systems began to be developed with increasingly sophisticated interfaces in the form of software agents that could interact directly with learners. The second half of the 1990s saw a preponderance of pedagogical agents, often taking the form of screen-based animated characters. These agents were designed to motivate learners by providing social cues through their gestures, expressions, voices and actions. Whereas some agents took the guise of animated animals, aliens or robots, many were programmed to assume realistic human appearances. The idea of agents talking and behaving like a real person has long been seen as a means to increase learner engagement and empathy. As one leading developer put it, human-like software agents 'add social elements that great teachers often employ'.[5]

Developing convincing pedagogical agents is a complicated undertaking. As well as the sophisticated numerical modelling of 'expert knowledge' and 'learner knowledge', the design of any agent interface involves various decisions regarding 'who' the agent is to 'be'.[6] Alongside the agent's visual and auditory appearance are nuanced questions of character, personality and emotional state. For example, how competent should the agent be? Should it come across as sympathetic or authoritarian? Much attention is also given to 'detailed design' options such as the agent's age, gender, ethnicity and personal background. Unlike character building in other areas of software development, significant planning is required for bringing even the most rudimentary of teacher agents to life.

A range of decisions also arise regarding what sort of teaching style and approach the agent will adopt. Here, most developers tended to pursue a preference for 'tutor' style agents where reasoning is shared between users and the machine.[7] This style of 'one-to-one tutoring' is summed up in the 'INSPIRE' dictum – i.e. 'intelligent, nurturant, Socratic, progressive, indirect, reflective and encouraging'.[8] As noted in Chapter 1, many developers consider these characteristics as significantly superior to the experience of mass classroom instruction. Art Graesser – one of the pioneers in the field – started his work on pedagogical agents by analysing over 100 hours of videoed lessons from teachers who were untrained in tutoring techniques. This led to the conclusion that 'normal' teachers 'are not prone to implement sophisticated tutoring strategies that have been proposed in the fields of education, the learning sciences, and developers of ITSs'.[9]

One defining aspect of pedagogical agents is their capacity for sense-making and autonomous action, distinguishing them from software that simply delivers programmed responses.[10] In striving to produce agents that can sense their environments and then act upon this information in autonomous (rather than scripted) ways, developers began to explore the innovative application of AI techniques. For example, advances in knowledge representation, computational linguistics, planning and vision were used throughout the 2000s to give agents the capacity to estimate 'what learners know, feel and can do'.[11] These techniques were also used to allow agents to work out what teaching techniques have worked previously for the learner and then scaffold subsequent learning accordingly.

Various agents were developed in this manner throughout the 1990s, 2000s and 2010s. Graesser and colleagues in the University of Memphis developed a series of well-regarded AutoTutor intelligent systems. These made extensive use of natural language processing, and involved various pedagogical agents developed to support conversational learning in areas such as algebra, psychology and critical thinking. AutoTutor agents – usually presented in the form of an animated head and shoulders – could ask questions and follow up on misunderstandings with relevant hints and prompts (so-called 'Expectation-Misconception-Tailored' dialogue).

Another celebrated pedagogical agent at the time was Steve (Soar Training Expert for Virtual Environments).[12] This was an animated agent with head, arms and upper body, designed to act as a knowledgeable member of a team. Steve could demonstrate and explain physical procedural tasks, and then monitor and assist other team members as they learnt to perform the tasks. Alongside Steve were much-publicized agents such as Coach Mike (designed to tutor people in computer programming) and Herman (an animated bug that supported botanical tuition). Also of note were the University of Southern

California's life-size twin sisters designed to educate visitors to the Boston Museum of Science. Ada and Grace were programmed to 'banter' with visitors, talk about their home lives and boyfriends, and occasionally display 'signs of sibling rivalry'. As the developers explained, these twins 'were expressly designed in this way to appeal to children and young teens'.[13]

Current trends in pedagogical agents

While impressive for their time, much of this initial wave of pedagogical agents relied on what, at best, could be described as 'narrow' or 'weak' AI capabilities. Recently, however, agents are benefiting from continuing advances in areas of AI such as vision processing and natural language processing. One key advance is the ability to gather large amounts of data about learners and learning environments. This includes capturing data relating to learners' gaze, posture, and even electrical activity in the brain. Such data now allow intelligent tutoring systems to use machine learning methods to infer what learners are thinking and how they feel, and to predict what they are likely to do next. In addition, natural language processing and speech recognition technology has advanced to the point of supporting 'more natural tutorial dialogue'.[14] Developers of systems such as Alelo's Enskill now make bold claims to support artificially intelligent on-screen characters capable of 'authentic' communication.[15]

Underpinning these advances is the idea of agents that can recognize and react to human emotions and moods. This is described by some developers as aligning the system with each learner's 'traits' and 'states'.[16] There are a number of ways in which agents are now able to be affect-sensitive and pick up on excitement, boredom, anger or confusion in the people they are working with. For example, increasing use is being made of data generated by facial recognition, eye-tracking and other biometric techniques of mood detection. In addition, some agents are now designed to 'mine' data from learners' engagement with 'empathy technologies' such as social media, which tend to generate emotionally charged data.

At the same time, a range of AI techniques are being used to engineer agents that display their own emotions, what developers term affect synthesis. The aim here is to design lifelike agents that are 'natural and believable'.[17] For example, developers talk of designing the 'heart, mind and nerves'[18] of an agent to allow it to intervene in learning processes and guide people toward system goals that might differ from what they would otherwise choose for themselves. Field trials continue to show the effectiveness of agents with emotional plausibility, with learners tending to quickly disengage when an online character's facial responses or tone of voice do not come across as realistic and congruent. Developers are increasingly confident of their ability to build 'emotionally intelligent' agents that are 'phenomenally responsive' to a learner's emotions.[19]

These advances are all driving a diversity in the types of role now being developed for these agents. Rather than acting as unflinching demonstrators or explainers, agents are now assuming various nuanced 'mentoring' approaches. These include agents that act in stoic 'butler' roles and even confrontational 'competitor' and 'trouble-maker' personas.[20] There is also considerable interest in developing so-called teachable agents that act as companions and near-peers which learners themselves are required to tutor and help. Some systems now use multiple agents to work with a single learner, all engaging in cross-agent interactions and sometimes disagreeing or contradicting each other. Agents are even being designed to replicate the appearance of the learner, thus requiring the individual to teach a 'digital doppelganger' of themselves.[21]

This new generation of agents is being applied across a range of topics and knowledge areas, from teamwork tutoring to cultural sensitivity training. Advances in body sensors and smart-glass technology are allowing the development of agents that support complex psychomotor and movement-based learning such as rifle marksmanship and orienteering. A recent ambition amongst developers is to design agents that have 'life-long' and 'life-wide' relationships with individuals, rather than being used only for episodic experiences.[22] The idea here is that individuals can develop long-term relationships with their agent, while the system can collate longitudinal data relating to how the person learns in different situations. Developers talk of people building rapport and trust with these lifelong learning companions – 'forging on-going relationships with them, just as people do'.[23]

The potential and practicalities of pedagogical agents

The ongoing development of pedagogical agents and intelligent tutoring certainly fits with the idea of learning as a fundamentally social process. As William Swartout argues, learning with these agents 'becomes much like interacting with a real person and this can bring social elements to the interaction that are not easily supported with conventional interfaces'.[24] It is claimed that people find interacting with pedagogical agents to be an 'engrossing' experience that blurs reality and fantasy.[25] In particular, it is argued that pedagogical agents can be especially motivating for 'struggling' and 'lower ability' learners.[26] Intelligent tutoring systems are described as 'safe environments for learners',[27] where learning tasks can be repeated *ad infinitum*.

Researchers and developers in the field of intelligent tutoring are certainly confident of the effectiveness of these systems. Yet, at best, it is accepted that well-designed agents can have a 'small but significant effect on learning'.[28] It has been suggested, for example, that agents might be more impactful with young learners,[29] that a majority of people react better to 'chatty' rather than 'serious' agents, and that teenage boys prefer to work with expert agents rather than peer agents. Nevertheless, there is limited robust evidence that might be able to point to the sustained educational impacts of these technologies. For the time being, peda-gogical agents tend to be justified primarily in terms of their cost-effectiveness, convenience and consistency.

The most common question asked by those working outside the field of intelligent tutoring is what impli-cations these technologies might have for human teachers. In response, developers are keen to stress that their products largely complement rather than threaten the job of a human teacher. It is argued that agents can provide sustained attention and support to a majority of learners, with teachers freed-up for individuals in need of specialist attention. Pedagogical agents can fulfil an important 'triaging' role, with system data from a group of agent-assisted learners increasing the capacity of a teacher to know what is taking place across a classroom. As Johnson and Lester reason, 'pedagogical agents complement the roles of humans in the learning process and should not be viewed as taking the place of them'.[30]

Despite such assurances, there is a notable emphasis throughout intelligent tutoring research and development on the primacy of one-to-one tutors and mentors. In this sense, some developers certainly envisage their agents doing away with the conventional classroom teacher directing a class of students on her own. As Art Graesser put it, 'It could be argued that tutoring was the very first form of instruction. Children were trained one-on-one by parents, other relatives, and members of the village who had particular specialized skills. The apprenticeship model reigned for several millennia before we encountered the industrial revolution and classroom education.'[31] Clearly, the implementation of pedagogical agents is associated with ambitions to fundamentally alter the nature of traditional forms of teaching and learning as developed in schools, universities and other education institutions. In this regard, there are a number of broader issues that need to be explored.

A reduced synthetic experience?

First are questions of authenticity and depth of experience. All the systems and agents described in this chapter primarily support virtual representations of teaching. In theory, virtual agents are cheap to provide, and can support consistent, reliable teaching that is easily controlled and monitored. However, in theory, virtual technologies *also* offer the possibility to move beyond the limitations of real-life practices and processes, and allow learners to experience situations that otherwise would not be possible. Here, there is less sense of pedagogical agents extending the realms of learning and moving beyond what learners might otherwise experience. Besides the gimmick of talking to a bug, living on a space-station or teaching a computer-generated doppelganger, these systems mostly provide rudimentary replications of familiar 'real-life' learning processes and practices. Steve might well be able to walk someone through how to operate an air compressor on board a ship, but he is unlikely to lead them into otherwise unimaginable realms.

If anything, the forms of computer-based tutoring outlined in this chapter can be seen as abbreviated, bounded and ultimately reduced versions of fairly routine educational processes and practices. Key here is the limited nature of any interaction that a learner can expect to have with their 'tutor'. As Campanelli and colleagues note, despite the 'founding myth' of interactivity, virtual technologies are only capable of offering the user an 'infinite number of finite options'.[32] An off-hand mention of Shakespeare is unlikely to trigger Herman The Bug to reflect on the influence of sixteenth-century art on botanical knowledge. Similarly, it could be argued that most aspects of human interaction can only be crudely simulated and approximated. It is difficult to describe how a teenage girl engages in 'banter' or how a butler might smile wryly. As such, it is incredibly difficult to automate and simulate these processes. All these intelligent systems and agents are essentially scripted and configured along limited lines. This can make interacting with such virtual technologies a frustratingly 'castrated' experience, offering 'synthetic' rather than 'virtual' experiences of real-life encounters with teachers and teaching.[33]

These systems invariably reduce any act of learning to an individual's ability to respond to sets of pre-determined prompts and pre-programmed procedures. Even the most complex intelligent system is essentially built around closed forms of repetitive training. Despite claims of open-ended and socially rich learning, these systems are most successfully navigated along rational and repetitive lines. The ideal tutee of any intelligent tutoring system is someone who can adapt themselves to the expectations and requirements of the system in order to progress. In this sense, many learners will understandably attempt to 'game' their interactions with an agent – i.e. engage with the procedures in a strategic and calculated manner in order to trigger the 'correct' outcomes.

Despite the apparent complexity, diversity and creative design, any episode of agent-driven tutoring is invariably reduced to getting to know the system and being able to interpret and work with its coded logic – what could be termed a form of 'algorithmic mastery'. This certainly raises questions over the types of learning that are best supported through this technology. Even the systems that drive the most chatty agent interface could be said to facilitate little more than elaborate forms of information delivery and/ or 'behaviourist' training. As Audrey Watters put it, these are technologies built upon the principle of 'manipulat[ing] and influenc[ing] users, encouraging certain actions or behaviors and discouraging others and cultivating a kind of "addiction" or conditioned response'.[34] This might be appropriate for *some* types of skills development, but it is clearly a limited means of fostering many other forms of understanding, knowledge and sense-making.

Manipulating individual action

As with most AI-driven efforts to automate teaching, any intelligent tutoring system or pedagogical agent is essentially a form of individually focused behaviour management – what is sometimes termed 'nudging' people's decision-making and action. This approach relates to the basic belief (originating from the field of 'behavioural economics') that people often act in irrational ways and make ill-considered decisions that are not in their best interests.[35] This approach now guides efforts in many areas of everyday life to affectively manipulate the psychology of choice – that is, influencing an individual's instincts, emotions, impulses and evolved cultural habits. By monitoring and measuring these traits, it is reasoned that they can be manipulated and altered as a means of managing future decisions and actions.

The 'nudge' mentality is increasingly used to justify the ongoing adoption of pedagogical agents and other forms of AI-based 'guidance' in education. Indeed, talk of nudging is now evident across many aspects of contemporary life – from commercial advertising through to urban design and public health policies – to intervene in what people do while maintaining a sense of individual autonomy and self-control. This growing interest in data-informed self-regulation reflects a particularly neoliberal approach to improving learning. Successful engagement with learning is framed as resulting from the choices and freedoms of individuals, with individuals considered the primary source of educational improvement. While the field of intelligent CAI emerged long before the prominence of such thinking, the current generation of pedagogical agents is being implemented along these very lines.

Such principles raise a number of problems implicit in the idea of individually focused, affectively centred tutoring. First is the argument that people are not always able to act in agentic ways and simply 'change' their behaviours when given appropriate feedback. For example, one's 'states' and 'traits' are not wholly self-determined, and certainly not always related to the current moment. There are many reasons why an individual might come to a learning episode in an angry or distracted state that no amount of responsive feedback from a pedagogical agent will alter. The increased onus on the individual to improve their learning performance also increases the self-responsibilization of risk when improvements do not occur. Positioning learning in this way unfairly marginalizes the many structural issues that might prevent some individuals from effectively 'engaging' and progressing. Learning is not a straightforward process that all individuals have ultimate control over.

It can also be argued that relying on software agents for prompts and guidance does not necessarily make individuals stronger in terms of making future decisions for themselves. As Nick Seaver argues, algorithmic recommender systems are primarily designed to 'hook' people into frequent or enduring usage – what Seaver describes as 'traps' rather than prompts to move on to something else.[36] Similarly, then, learning by being 'guided' what to do by a machine is likely to lead some people to assume a passive manipulable approach to learning in the future. Having one's instincts shaped and nudged can be a depowering and infantilizing experience for some people – preventing them from thinking for themselves. In this sense, there is much about having constant monitoring from a lifelong learning agent that could be ultimately unhelpful.

The ethical dilemma of the robot teacher

Pedagogical agents also raise ethical issues similar to those covered in Chapter 2. For example, the idea of encouraging young and vulnerable learners to form social bonds and an emotional rapport with on-screen agents in the guise of a tutor or teacher clearly raises concerns over deception. There are a number of ethical issues relating to 'mental privacy', not least the constant prospect of having what once were private emotions and inner psychological traits now made a focus of public attention and public property.

The idea of deploying pedagogical agents in classrooms to direct teachers' attention to particular students also raises an ethical issue relevant to many different forms of AI use in education. As debates in areas such as self-driving cars and drone warfare show, any 'autonomous' decision is value-laden in its logic and its outcomes. This is neatly illustrated in the so-called 'Ethical Dilemma of Self-Driving Cars' thought experiment, which describes an autonomous vehicle having to make a last-minute decision over which occupants of a busy pedestrian-crossing to crash into. Every machine-based action has consequences and side-effects for users and 'non-users'. Some people get to benefit more than others.

So, what might an educational equivalent of this dilemma be when applied to more mundane decisions within the day-to-day life of the classroom? Here we might imagine a number of scenarios based on the dilemma: 'Which students does the pedagogical agent direct the classroom teacher to help?' For example, who does the intelligent system tell the teacher to help first – the struggling student who rarely attends school and is predicted to fail, or a high-flying 'top of the class' student? Alternatively, what logic should lie behind deciding whether to direct the teacher toward a group of students who are clearly coasting, or a solitary student who seems to be excelling? What if this latter student is in floods of tears? Perhaps there might be a third option focused on the well-being of the teacher. For example, should the agent choose to ignore the students needing help and direct a weary teacher to take time-out to summon up some extra energy and regain composure?

This ethical dilemma neatly illustrates the limitations of automated decision-making in educational settings. Interestingly, most teachers quickly get frustrated when asked to engage in educational versions of the dilemma.

Teachers complain that these scenarios seem insultingly simplistic. There are a range of other factors that one needs to know in order to make an informed decision. In particular, all the factors that are *not* included in the dilemma point to the complexity of devising algorithms that might be considered appropriate for a real-life classroom. Whom a teacher chooses to help at any one moment in a classroom can be a split-second decision based on intuition, a broader contextual knowledge about the student, and a general 'feel' for what might be going on in the class. There can be a host of counter-intuitive factors that prompt a teacher to go with their gut feeling rather than what is considered to be professional 'best practice'. These 'dilemmas' are something that any human teacher will encounter hundreds of times each day, and their responses will be based on experience developed over time. What other teachers 'should do' in similar predicaments is unlikely to be something that can be written down, let alone codified into a set of rules for all teachers to follow. These are very significant issues to be attempting to calculate, predict and engineer.

Conclusions

Regardless of these criticisms, pedagogical agents and intelligent tutoring systems are sophisticated technologies that perform well in specific conditions and contexts. Yet the question of whether intelligent tutors and pedagogical agents could be used to teach across school systems or workforces on a broad scale is complex. These technologies certainly do not seem to fit effortlessly with *all* types of teaching and learning. Indeed, it is telling that the development of intelligent tutoring in the US continues to be driven significantly by military and industry funding – contexts where some of the concerns raised in this chapter are perhaps of less relevance. For example, issues of emotional privacy or self-responsibilities for failure might apply differently to military personnel than to young school children. The suggestion of intelligent tutoring being rolled out across education systems needs to be taken seriously. If we are going to allow ourselves to have a 'learning companion' for life then we need to think carefully about what we are letting ourselves in for. Having a 'virtual Socrates' hovering constantly in the background might not be as inspiring as it sounds.

It is now time to again shift our attention toward another set of technologies. Chapters 2 and 3 have considered technologies that are explicitly configured as alternative 'teachers'. A pedagogical agent or robot teacher is clearly positioned as a fully formed equivalent to a human teacher. Yet perhaps the most pervasive uses of AI in education are teaching technologies that purport to work 'behind the scenes'. The next chapter will consider a range of AI-driven technologies now finding their way into education settings that seek to automate specific procedures and practices that previously would have been directed by a human teacher. As Chapter 4 will go on to discuss, various AI-driven technologies now deal with student queries, plan teaching activities, assess assignments, keep classes 'engaged' and generally support educational provision. Taken as a whole, these technologies could be seen to cast doubt on the need for professionally trained expert 'teachers'. At the very least, they raise the question of whether the people who are now working alongside these technologies should be considered as 'teachers' at all.

FOUR

'Behind-the-Scenes' Technologies

Pedagogical agents and physical robots certainly fit what most people might immediately imagine as 'robots replacing teachers'. In contrast, this chapter explores various 'behind-the-scenes' AI-driven technologies that are also designed to carry out work that would otherwise be carried out by a human teacher. These include advances in personalized learning, learning analytics and other facets of the fast-growing learning sciences. Also of note are administrative-focused technologies designed to dispense advice to students, assess work, plan lessons and even direct teachers in what to say and do. All told, computers are increasingly becoming involved in decision-making and actions that human teachers might have previously considered to be routine elements of their job.

While these technologies might appear to be innovative, it is important to remember that such efforts stretch back well into the twentieth century. For example, there are clear parallels with the programmed instruction technologies introduced into schools from the

1920s onwards. Early instances of programmed instruction techniques included mechanical multiple-choice machines and chemo-sheets where learners checked their answers with chemical-dipped swabs. Perhaps the most celebrated of these technologies were the Teaching Machines of the 1950s and 1960s. These were automated desktop boxes that divided learning processes into successions of very small steps, with positive reinforcement dispensed with the successful accomplishment of each step. As the psychologist B. F. Skinner (one of the pioneers of teaching machines) observed, 'there is no reason why the schoolroom should be any less mechanized than, for example, the kitchen'.[1]

Alongside these attempts to relieve teachers from the burdens of instructing learners, automated technologies have long been developed to support bureaucratic and administrative aspects of teaching. Inventions such as the Pressey Testing Machine of the 1920s were praised in their time for freeing teachers from the 'drudgery' of the many administrative and organizational aspects of the job.[2] While these pre-digital machines usually relied on rudimentary analog mechanics, some of the issues raised by such attempts at educational automation hold true for today's AI-driven digital equivalents – not least the numerous implications of these technologies for the role and status of the classroom teacher.

Digital automations of contemporary teaching

Instead of chemical swabs and punch-cards, the current wave of automated classroom technologies reflects the digitally infused nature of contemporary education provision. For example, the ubiquity of personal digital devices (not least smartphones, tablets and laptops) ensures that most schools and universities operate in a state of 'one-to-one' access where every student and teacher has access to at least one personal device at any time. This allows educational institutions to operate through large-scale platforms, such as the all-encompassing 'learning management system'. At the same time, students and teachers are making frequent use of social media, apps and other online services. Crucially, all these technologies facilitate the continuous generation and processing of large quantities of data. This data relates to most aspects of education – ranging from the individual actions of students and teachers to institution-wide processes and 'performance'. While some of this data is deliberately generated for analytic purposes, vast amounts of 'naturally occurring' data also arise from the daily use of school systems, personal devices and other technologies.

As discussed in previous chapters, this increased scale and scope of data in education lends itself to sophisticated forms of automation. Indeed, schools and universities are being steadily reorganized around the exhaustive amounts of detailed data that are now generated through digital technology use, with educators welcoming the speed and flexibility in how this data is produced and processed, alongside the wide range of data types and sources that now exist.[3] Coupled with advances in the forms of data generation and processing outlined in previous chapters (such as machine learning techniques and natural language processing), we are now seeing various forms of data-driven automation of previously human-led processes, practices and tasks. Altogether, data-driven digital technologies are now doing a lot of what might otherwise be expected from a classroom teacher. These include the following four types of application.

Personalized learning systems

First is the growth of personalized learning systems that direct students' engagement with online learning resources. This is software designed to support the adaptive sequencing of education resources in light of a learner's previous performance. Whereas the pedagogical agents described in Chapter 3 work within a single intelligent tutoring system, these personalized learning systems are designed to guide individuals through many different online sources of learning. One popular example of this logic is the Knewton 'adaptive learning system'. This is an online 'recommender' system that uses large-scale data techniques to calculate what particular segment of online learning each of its enrolled students should be using. Once a student is logged onto a course or tutorial through the Knewton system, the platform's data engine monitors every interaction that the individual has with the computer. This data is used to model various aspects of the learner's performance, such as their motivation and proficiency, as well as estimations of 'learning style'. These learning profiles are then used to recommend the most appropriate educational resource that the student should use next. Each learner benefits from the vast quantity of data being analysed, purportedly in excess of one million data points per person. This is claimed to give Knewton the capability to know more about any individual's learning than a real-life teacher could ever hope to know.

Many of these data-driven adaptive systems are designed to complement (or even compensate for) the learning that takes place in school. For example, the Chinese YiXue Corporation has established over 1,500 adaptive learning centres where their proprietary

AI-driven personalized learning system can be used by students before and after school hours. For additional fees, these centres offer the option of supplementary support from an online tutor *or* an in-person tutor. The YiXue platform makes innovative use of natural language processing and emotion detection technology to determine the path that each student should follow. The company reckons that this results in its students achieving superior scores in China's rigorous annual Gaokao university entrance exams when compared to students coached by experienced human teachers. In the intensively competitive world of Chinese schooling, this is proving to be a major selling-point to families looking to gain an advantage for their children.

Learning analytics applications

Systems such as Knewton and YiXue are closely related to the areas of learning analytics and educational data-mining that have emerged over the past decade or so. Here developers are interested in applying computa-tional science and data science techniques to make sense of data relating to students, teachers and their immedi-ate educational contexts.[4] Specific areas of attention include the use of digital data to help students, teach-ers and institutions make informed decisions about teaching and learning.[5] This often involves making use of data arising from learning management systems, management information systems, student feedback, attendance data, location tracking and other sources of data generation. Learning analytics is therefore centred on the development of tools and techniques relating to data visualization, data integration, predictive modelling and classroom orchestration.

Many forms of learning analytics are now being used across schools and universities to provide analysis and insight into student performance that students can then use to plan their next moves. Often these take the form of simple dashboards and other visualizations that summarize students' performance, allow for comparisons with other learners and point to areas of improvement. More sophisticated Student Success Systems use data to predict student performance based on what is known about their previous engagement with course content, online interactions with students and teachers, and final assessment results. These systems also provide diagnoses of the factors likely to be influencing student under-performance and retention. An emerging area of multimodal analytics seeks to track how teachers and students move around a classroom, measuring noise levels and monitoring speech to gain a sense of how classroom interactions might be more evenly orchestrated.[6] As well as guiding the actions of individual students and their teachers, the aggregation of these types of data at an institutional level is seen to give schools and universities actionable forms of 'business intelligence' to inform strategic management and planning.

Guidance and advice chat-bots

Alongside these teaching and learning systems are efforts to automate general interactions that teachers might have with students. In particular, a number of universities have begun to explore the use of dialogue systems and conversational agents (commonly known as chat-bots) to field student queries and problems. In contrast to the pedagogical agents discussed in Chapter 3, these bots are intended to relieve teaching staff of having to deal with queries and interactions not related directly to learning. For example, IBM Watson (an AI system designed to answer questions) has been used as a basis for automated question-and-answer tutors on Georgia Tech postgraduate courses. In one early trial, students could choose to interact with nine online tutors, one of which was a bot named Jill Watson. The system was data-trained on a corpus of forum posts from previous classes and only permitted to respond if it was 97 per cent (or more) confident in its answer. Any questions that the system could not respond to were passed on to human instructors. Students continued to ask Jill questions throughout the course, relating to the scheduling of classes, assignment due dates and other logistical requirements. Reportedly, students had not guessed Jill's status by the end of the semester, 'although the impressive promptness of her responses aroused some suspicion'.[7]

Similarly, Deakin University in Australia has been using IBM Watson as the basis for student chat-bots that deal with questions regarding campus-based issues. This software reportedly fields around 1,600 questions per week, with commonly asked queries including 'How do I meet other students from my course?', 'Where can I get food on campus?', 'When is my exam?' and 'Where is the library?' As well as being trained on previous student query data, the natural language processing system scours the university website to generate evidence-weighted answers. The university reports that its students are happy with the service. Indeed, a similar trial at the Technical University of Berlin found that a natural language chat-bot could halve students' time spent before the start of term organizing their classes when compared to using the university's standard online help system.

Automated essay grading

Another specialized instance of education automation is the area of automated essay assessment – so-called 'robo-grading'. While computers have long been used to automatically grade multiple-choice tests, developers now consider AI techniques capable of accurately grading written answers. Using machine learning techniques to process a mass corpus of essays graded by humans, these systems can learn to grade essays in terms of recognizing various features of the written text. This ranges from accuracy of spelling and grammar, through the pattern matching of the essay's topic focus, sentence structure, the appearance of coherent arguments, and the complexity of word choice. Essays can then be scored automatically alongside a confidence rating, with any essays marked with a low confidence score or borderline grade being flagged for reassessment by a human grader.

Developers see this technology as fulfilling a number of supportive roles in schools and universities. These include providing formative feedback on writing quality and a means of improving reading comprehension through summary writing.[8] Most notably, this technology is now attracting interest in terms of the growing prevalence of mass standardized high-stakes testing around the world. Pearson – one of the largest education companies in the world – reckon that they automatically grade around 34 million student essays from US state and national high-stakes tests each year. This relies on using a machine learning system which assesses essays in terms of 100 different features. While these systems make no judgement of writing creativity and artistry, developers reason that the computer does exactly what human teachers would have done previously. As Tovia Smith puts it, 'purists may turn their nose up at that kind of formulaic writing, but . . . the computers learn what good writing is from teachers, and just mirror that'.[9]

The potential and practicalities of automated educational software

These examples highlight the diversity of teaching tasks that AI-driven technologies are now assuming responsibility for. In essence, these are all tasks that previously would have been the preserve of education professionals. Now, these technologies promise to undertake the work at speeds and scales that no human teacher could ever achieve. The pressing question arising from these various technologies is straightforward enough:

Just what are education professionals now supposed to be doing? Why will we continue to need expensively trained, specialist human teachers in the near future?

Despite the growing capacity of such technologies, very few people are expecting the complete removal of human oversight from the education process. All of the technologies just described involve a degree of input from tutors, mentors and other classroom assistants. Indeed, some of these systems are being justified as enhancing rather than threatening the status of the expert teacher. In this sense, there are many practical reasons for these technologies and systems to be welcomed by classroom teachers. After all, many teachers are definitely over-worked and stressed, and it is increasingly difficult to provide all students with full levels of support at all times. Who would not want to work slightly fewer hours? Who would not want more information and support in making decisions? Who would not want to be relieved of the burden of routine tasks?

As with the physical robots and pedagogical agents covered in Chapters 2 and 3, many of the technologies described in this chapter are justified as taking on tasks that otherwise distract teachers from essential teaching work. This idea of technology relieving rather than replacing the teacher is certainly not a new premise. Even the 1950s' 'teaching machines' described earlier were promoted as a way of freeing teachers to engage in 'proper' forms of work. As B. F. Skinner argued: 'Will machines replace teachers? On the contrary, they are capital equipment to be used by teachers to save time and labor.'[10] Such arguments continue to be made today. For example, it is claimed that learning analytics applications provide teachers with a 'conceptual exoskeleton' – an effective means of doing much of the 'heavy lifting' involved in scaling teacher efforts to large groups of learners. As Abelardo Pardo puts it, 'perhaps instructor expertise can be enhanced by technology in the same way that exoskeletons allow workers in factories to guide a rigid frame to manipulate extremely heavy objects'.[11]

The idea of the technologically enhanced teacher is an understandably attractive prospect. Yet these reconfigurations come with obvious implications for teachers and the education profession. One issue to consider here is the growing trend of 'teacher-proofing' classroom processes through the use of digital technologies so that no expert decision-making is required. For example, however 'teacher-friendly' they might appear, these technologies are often deployed in ways that are directive rather than directable. In other words, they are designed to make decisions and provide clear guidance for learners and their teachers. Indeed, one of the key selling-points of personalized and adaptive learning approaches is their capacity to guide any non-specialist 'teacher' through what the learner should be doing.

In a similar manner to the classroom application of pedagogical agents discussed in Chapter 3, these are systems that are designed to make pedagogical decisions, with teachers then expected to help enact these decisions. With this in mind, some people are being led to argue that the job of a 'teacher' might become more like a generalist 'proctor' or 'technician'. Conversely, perhaps highly trained professional teachers will no longer need organization and managerial skills in areas such as curriculum planning, pedagogical design and diagnosis of learning difficulties. So, why might this *not* be a good thing? Here, we can raise a number of questions about data integrity, the fairness of individualized and personalized learning, and the implications of these technologies in terms of labour politics.

Holding data to account

First are questions about the data that lies beneath these data-driven technologies and the appropriateness of what is being done with it. Key here are issues of data integrity and robustness. For example, how representative is this data? How reductive is it? What does it *not* tell us about the social and cultural dimensions of education, teaching and learning? These questions all point to concerns over what is being measured and calculated by these systems. Underpinning these concerns, then, is an uncertainty about the rearranging of classrooms and schools along data-driven lines. Regardless of the power of Big Data, it can be argued that classrooms are not closed, computable systems based upon controllable variables that can be monitored and manipulated. Instead, they are complex, messy places where much that happens cannot be easily monitored and measured. Students lead complicated lives that are not neatly described and accounted for, let alone captured and calculated. Indeed, it could be argued that there are not enough data points in the world to adequately capture the complexities and nuances of who a student is, or how a school functions.

From this perspective, any attempt to model educational processes along data-driven lines clearly needs to be subjected to basic questions of values and bias. Put bluntly, if automation means following a set of rules then three obvious points of contention arise: (i) what rules are being followed? (ii) whose rules are they?, and (iii) what values and assumptions do they reflect? Like any rule-making process, algorithms do not magically fall out of the sky. Somebody somewhere sets down a series of complex coded instructions and protocols to be repeatedly followed. Yet in a world of proprietary platforms and impenetrable coding, this logic typically remains imperceptible to most non-specialists. This is why people often apply the catering industry euphemism of 'secret sauce' when talking about algorithms that drive search engines, news feeds and content recommendations. Something in these recipes certainly seems to hit the spot, but only very few people are 'in the know' as to exactly what the calculations are.

Such secrecy might be an effective strategy when selling fast-food, but it perhaps sits less comfortably with the ethos of supporting people to learn. Crucially, if using an automated system entails following someone else's logic then, by extension, this also means being subject to their values, ideas and politics. Even the most innocuous logic of [IF X THEN Y] is not a neutral, value-free calculation. Any programmed action is based on pre-determined understandings of what X and Y are, and what their relation to each other might be. Such understandings are shaped by the pre-existing ideas, ideals and intentions of programmers, as well as the cultures and contexts in which these programmers are situated. So, the key question to ask of any automated educational system is *who* is now being trusted to program the teaching? Most importantly, *what* are their values and ideas about education? In implementing any digital system, what choices and decisions are now being pre-programmed into our classrooms?

The inequalities of individualization

Questions can also be asked about the logic of personalization and the centring of education around the calculated needs of each individual learner. Most of the technologies outlined in Chapters 3 and 4 follow an ideal of personalized learning. As Anthony Seldon puts it, 'everyone can have the very best teacher and it's completely personalized; the software you're working with will be with you throughout your education journey'.[12] Rather than following the same lessons as their peers, personalized learning systems and learning analytics give students the responsibility for organizing, directing and controlling their own learning activities as they see fit. This certainly contrasts with the 'paternalistic' expectation of many formal courses that all students will use the same tools and have the same interactions – largely orchestrated and arranged by the teacher.

These shifts have some substance behind them. For example, theories of self-regulated learning highlight the importance of individuals being able to continually monitor their own progress, identify strengths and weaknesses, and plan strategic ways forward to adapt and improve. This reflexive state of educational engagement is seen to depend upon individuals receiving frequent feedback about their learning. Similarly, this also fits with a general shift across most aspects of everyday life toward what has been termed 'networked individualism'.[13] Now, people are increasingly using social and networked technologies to dip in and out of loosely knit social circles of other networked individuals. These are all highly personal arrangements with the individual placed at the centre.

Such individualized approaches may well have merit, but they also have clear limitations. Aside from the altered role of the teacher (which we shall discuss below), there are a number of concerns relating to the likely injustices of the individualized learning taking place through these technologies. Most notably, the expectation of *everyone* being able to exercise a genuinely free choice in their engagement with education is naive, if not disingenuous. One does not have to be a sociologist to recognize that we live in 'structured' social environments where choices are bounded, contained and tempered by who we are. Of course, an individual can strive to influence the ways in which their 'fate' plays out through hard work, training and cultivating their talents. Yet what someone can realistically 'choose' to do remains dictated by a combination of individual efforts *and* broader social circumstances. All the forms of 'choice' provided by the technologies outlined in this chapter are clearly going to benefit some individuals more than others.

Any discussion of these technologies therefore has to question the extent to which the idea of the self-responsibilized, self-determining learner advantages those individuals who are able to act in agentic, self-motivated, empowered ways. While AI-driven education might work well for individuals, it is likely to work better for some individuals rather than others. At best, then, it is likely that only privileged groups will be able to act in this empowered fashion. If we are all immersed in our own personalized learning journeys, what implications might this have for education as a social, supportive and shared endeavour? This is not to dismiss the technology-based personalization and individualization of learning as a completely 'bad thing'. Digital technology is undoubtedly a powerful means of supporting different people to do different things in different ways. Yet the question that arises is straightforward enough – to what extent is education compromised when reframed as a digitally based 'free-for-all'?

The labour politics of automated teaching

Finally, there are issues relating to the labour politics of education work. Most of the technologies outlined in this chapter are presented as enriching and enhancing the role of the human teacher. Proponents of technology-driven teaching are keen to argue that teachers are liberated to assume a more peripatetic role, much like a hospital consultant. Teachers may also have the time and space to provide more playful and provocative interventions. Yet an alternative scenario is teachers taking on less empowered, more administrative functions. In following the lead of these machines, it could be argued that teachers will themselves be pushed into working more like robots, with their classroom activities being diminished to a routinized, de-professionalized drudge.

These technologies certainly reframe the teacher's role as one of primarily stewarding the educational activities of students in ways that have already been decided and determined by machines. All of these technologies separate the tasks of teaching into different components, and diminish the ability of human teachers to exercise professional judgement and expertise over the process as a whole. Thus, the teacher is reduced to a role of interpreting and enacting the expert judgement of various automated elements of the classroom. A teacher may well have to think of explanations *why* a student received a particular grade on their 'robo-graded' essay, but they will not be responsible for giving that grade. A teacher may have to support a student through a particular learning task that they have been 'recommended' to do, but they may well not have a good sense of why this is an appropriate course of action. In essence, everything a teacher does is ultimately driven by coded decision-making processes. These are technologies designed to organize teaching and set the parameters of what can (and what cannot) be done.

There are a number of problems with this. First, it can be argued that much of what is being automated is actually an important aspect of the teacher's job. Some of the seemingly menial tasks of a teacher's day can actually be the more generative. For example, teachers may not necessarily relish grading essays, but most acknowledge that providing rich feedback on students' work is a key part of the teaching process. A student purporting to ask where they can get food on campus (when that information is already well-advertised online) might be a gateway to much richer conversations and cultural exchange, or perhaps a prompt to look into a student's welfare. It could be argued that delegating these tasks to machines detracts from the overall job of the teacher, rather than enhancing their professionalism.

Second, the routinization and fragmentation of teaching work can be seen as profoundly disempowering. Just as learners can be demotivated by being constantly 'nudged' what to do by pedagogical agents, teachers are also undermined by having machines guide and direct their every move. In the 1970s, social researchers like Harry Braverman pointed to the ways in which factory workers were progressively being 'deskilled' by the fragmentation of production-line processes, and the separation of the 'conception' of what they were doing from its 'execution'.[14] What would have once been a highly skilled craft job was now achieved on a factory production line by unskilled people working separately and repetitively on different things that they were directed to do. It could be argued that similar forms of alienation continue through the digital mechanization of teaching work.

Finally, there are concerns over the weakening of organized labour. In short, if teaching is recast as a non-specialized role based primarily around stewarding technology and students, then this has likely implications for the hiring and firing of teachers. With less need to recruit and retain highly trained professionals, education managers and administrators will be able to employ cheaper workers with generalized organizational and clerical skills. These 'efficiencies' raise a host of questions regarding the de-professionalization of teaching, not least concerning which teachers are likely to be 'let go' as a consequence. Will automated teaching turn out to be an indirect opportunity to get rid of expensive older teachers, or troublesome unionized teachers? Is automated teaching an underhand means of getting rid of those who cannot adopt flexible working patterns, for example women and care-givers? These technologies certainly do not appear to bode well for *every* person who is currently a trained teaching professional.

Conclusions

Teachers' work in educational institutions is becoming increasingly automated through the types of digital technology outlined in this chapter. It can certainly be argued that these technologies all work to make aspects of teaching more 'efficient' – that is, more reliable, consistent, standardized and cheap. Yet these technologies also change the character of the education settings that they are used in. If an automated essay grading system awards high marks for a particular narrative style, argument structure and word sequencing, then this is the kind of writing that people are likely to produce. If an automated chat-bot can only respond to questions relating to content taken from a university's website, then this determines the types of help that can be provided. These technologies support consistent, standardized and controllable versions of education. Yet in making school and university learning a 'teacher-proof' process, are we also stripping away some of the essential qualities of education? Perhaps there is something to be said for uncertainty, serendipity and organized chaos?

The past three chapters have covered a range of sophisticated examples of AI-driven education. These innovations raise a diversity of issues, arguments and concerns. On the positive side, we have seen recurring hopes of using AI tools and techniques to drive the expansion of education at scale and at speed. Powerful data-processing techniques offer the chance to analyse learning data and provide guidance, direction and support on a systematic, consistent and reliable basis. Key here is a desire to place more control in the hands of individual learners – allowing people to learn in more personalized and flexible ways. However, more worryingly, we have also seen recurring concerns over ethics, inequalities, injustices and the clear limitations of 'data and algorithms to address social problems that are incredibly complex'.[15] We have also touched upon the unintended consequences of these technologies – not least in diminishing the humanity of educational practices. The final chapter therefore returns to some of the central questions raised in Chapter 1. What can we now say about the likely implications of the technologies and techniques that we have covered in this book? How might we want to challenge (and possibly rethink) this technology and how it is implemented in education settings? Given the continued development of AI technology over the next decade or so, what kind of education do we want for the 2020s and beyond?

FIVE

Revitalizing Teaching for the AI Age

As the past four chapters have illustrated, there are few clear-cut answers when it comes to AI in education. These are technologies with obvious potential to substantially change many aspects of teaching. Which human teacher would not want to have 1,000 essays graded in a minute, or have a real-time overview of every student's performance? Yet, even these straight-forward promises come with considerable trade-offs and tensions. Are teachers being supported to work in 'smart' ways, or are their roles being irreversibly dumbed-down? Despite assurances to the contrary, many people might understandably feel that teachers are being pushed aside by these digital automations.

Such ambiguities remind us to approach AI and education in an appropriately critical manner. For example, when faced with confident predictions of benefits and transformations, it is always useful to also ask what is *not* being talked about. What is being sidelined, what is being lost? What is no longer being talked about in the same way? Without wanting to descend into dystopian visions of 'robots taking over the world', it is always useful to consider the undesirable things that might happen with any new technology. As Paul Virillo put it, 'when you invent the ship, you also invent the shipwreck'.[1]

As has been repeated throughout this book, we need to remain mindful of the socio-technical nature of AI and education. Any educational innovation involves likely reconfigurations of power, especially in terms of who gets to decide what 'teaching' and 'learning' is. While Saya, Knewton and Jill Watson are interesting technological artefacts in their own right, we need to pay close attention to the *ideas* and *interests* that lie behind them. All these technologies carry implicit assumptions about what education is, and in whose interests education operates. For example, many of the systems and applications described in this book imply continuous monitoring and measurement, 'nudging' decisions and changing individual behaviours, and the increased involvement of commercial actors. Is this *really* what we want future forms of education to look like?

In this spirit, we need to turn our attention away from specific systems and applications and instead concentrate on the social order that is being built around these technologies.[2] As such, the main issues that now need to be considered are not matters of engineering and design – that is, how to best develop software, calibrate algorithms or enhance the 'user experience'. Far more significant are the social, political, economic and cultural issues that surround these technologies. This raises important questions over fairness, disempowerment and what sort of future education provision we feel is appropriate. As such, there are no 'easy wins' or straightforward solutions that can be recommended. These are dilemmas that societies have grappled with for centuries, and will continue to face for a long time to come. This concluding chapter attempts to make sense of these complexities. There are some important choices to be made . . . so let's be sure that we know exactly what we are choosing!

What computers can (and can't) do in education

Regardless of the criticisms raised throughout this book, it is easy to see why many people consider AI to be a defining innovation of our time. These are highly sophisticated technological advances that are capable of powerful outcomes. For example, many AI-driven systems and applications are processing massive amounts of data to make connections and discern patterns that otherwise would not be identified.

These insights are used to construct sophisticated mathematical models of educational environments that allow for accurate future predictions. As we have seen, these insights can guide actions, direct resources and generally help teachers and learners to be better informed and prepared. All told, the capacities of AI technologies in education may already exceed those of humans – bringing a formal mathematical logic of 'calculability' to bear on teaching and learning situations that otherwise can only be dealt with through informed guesswork and speculative planning.

In this sense, the implementation of AI in education can be plausibly justified along a number of different lines. In pragmatic terms, AI-driven systems and applications cost less in the long term than training and employing humans to work as teachers. AI offers ways of delivering education that are likely to be more reliable, consistent and controllable. AI might also be seen to provide a basis for computationally precise, unambiguous decision-making. On a more abstract level, it can also be argued that AI technologies are capable of recognizing patterns and reaching decisions that humans would never consider. Indeed, one of the central claims of AI research is the capacity to identify essentially correct but completely 'unhuman' ways of doing things, as well as pointing to contentious trends and patterns that humans might prefer to overlook or ignore.

Nevertheless, this book has highlighted some clear limitations of AI technologies in education. In particular, these sophisticated computational processes are only as good as the data they are given. The past four chapters have pointed to plenty of instances where educational data might be inaccurate, incomplete, poorly chosen or simply a poor indicator of what it supposedly represents. These gaps and omissions are especially important in terms of modelling what teachers and learners do. Even the most complex models of 'teaching' and 'learning' contain significant grey areas. Moreover, there are many factors integral to understanding what goes on in education that may *never* be adequately measured and quantified. For example, how could one construct a genuinely nuanced and sensitive computation of a student's fragility or a realistic sense of family poverty? If data is the 'fuel' to the 'rocket engine' of AI, then these technologies risk being dangerously underpowered in terms of any capacity to make sense of education.

This leads to a problem that applies to all the technologies outlined in this book – a lack of common-sense understanding and nuanced awareness of educational contexts. On the one hand, there are plenty of data scientists and software developers who consider that *everything* is quantifiable, calculable and amenable to statistical control. On the other hand, there are many others who feel that education is one area of life where this logic is simply not appropriate. In particular, the reliance of AI on precision, clarity and predictability feels at odds with the many areas of education that rely on there being 'various shades of grey' and ambiguity. As Alexander Galloway argues, the primary 'problem with AI' is a problem of formalization.[3] As with written language or other formal symbolized systems, there are some things in education that cannot be fully captured and expressed through data processing – even if technically sophisticated approximations are possible. In a similar manner, Murray Goulden speaks of systems that are 'technologically smart' but also 'socially stupid', warning against our acceptance of technology that fails to 'understand the social practices it is attempting to appropriate'.[4]

Moreover, as with any instance of mathematical modelling, all AI technologies are built upon assumptions of acceptable levels of error and failure. As Adam Greenfield puts it, 'as long as the systems are "working" . . . any concern for mistaken results, whether it involves the production of false positives or false negatives, can be waved away as a quibble'.[5] Many educators might find it difficult to reconcile this stark mathematical logic with the process of helping others learn. Education is a context where teachers usually start from the premise of avoiding mis-diagnosis or wrong advice whenever possible.

The educational application of AI also suffers from an inevitable lack of explainability. In short, as AI systems become more complicated and further removed from simulated human intelligence, it is increasingly difficult to work out the rationales behind any decisions that these systems produce.[6] Even the programmers and engineers who design the current generation of machine learning systems soon struggle to isolate and explain the reasons that their system has for any particular action. Again, this logic sits uneasily with established ways of doing things in education. Teachers prefer to see themselves as well-informed 'reflexive' practitioners. Teaching and learning are considered to be processes where people need to know *why* as well as *what*. Simply being directed (or even instructed) what to do next does not constitute 'teaching' in its fullest sense.

Of course, none of these limitations should come as a surprise. Instead, they merely reflect the types of AI that we *actually* have in education, as opposed to the forms that are often speculated about. Fifty years since Hubert Dreyfus's treatise against 'Alchemy and

Artificial Intelligence',[7] AI remains an area of considerable hype and exaggeration. In reality, very few of the systems and applications described in this book make advanced use of the 'deep learning' techniques that are fuelling current enthusiasms for the potential of AI. It remains highly debatable whether we will *ever* see technology that comes close to achieving the much talked-about 'human-level AI' and artificial 'general' intelligence. In this sense, most of the grand promises currently being made on behalf of AI in education remain more speculative than substantial.

At best, then, the use of AI in education continues to take the form of what technologists term 'weak AI' or 'narrow AI'. These are systems that appear 'intelligent' only in terms of the specific tasks and predefined processes they are configured for. It is worth reminding ourselves that 'narrow' forms of AI are sophisticated technological developments that undoubtedly can play significant roles in education. These are certainly 'scrutable' in ways that more recent developments in advanced machine learning are not.[8] Yet these limitations need to be borne in mind before engaging in any discussion of what AI might 'do' for education. As Hilary Mason reminds us, AI is not 'magic' – instead 'it's math and data and computer programming, made by regular humans'.[9]

Restating the case for human teachers

Of course, many of the technological limitations noted throughout this book are undeniably applicable to human teachers. After all, human teachers make subjective decisions, are prone to misrecognition and bias, and can resort to manipulative practices and insincere displays of emotion. Furthermore (and to repeat a point made in Chapter 1), there are plenty of ineffectual and incompetent teachers who undoubtedly deserve to be replaced. AI developers and vendors might well consider their products to be merely as flawed as the human teachers already in the classroom. On this basis, some people are willing to consider that being 'as good as' a human teacher is justification enough for implementing these technologies in the classroom, particularly in situations where good teachers might be thin on the ground.

Yet this logic falls dangerously short of the basic rationales for the widespread implementation of AI in education. At this early stage of development, the aspirations of any attempt to deploy AI technologies in education need to be considerably grander than developing systems that are 'no worse' or 'slightly better' than the existing foibles and biases of human teachers.

Instead, advances in AI and other new technological domains are worth engaging with primarily in the expectation of *considerably* improving education. There is little sense in dedicating billions of dollars and millions of hours to produce systems that function along the same unsatisfactory lines as what is currently in place.

Moreover, there are plenty of other ways in which a good human teacher is clearly able to support learning that can *never* be fully replicated through technology. This echoes Edsger Dijkstra's observation that the question of 'can a machine think?' is equivalent to asking 'can a submarine swim?'[10] A submarine achieves many of the basic things that a fish does when swimming, but the two are hardly comparable in their intent or execution. In a similar manner, then, the question of whether machines can teach depends on how we choose to use the word 'teach'. On the basis of the past four chapters, there is plenty to suggest that the types of 'teaching' work supported by AI-based technologies are inherently limited in comparison to what a human teacher is capable of. Indeed, there are a number of qualities that should not be overlooked in the current rush toward automating the classroom.

First are the advantages that arise from human teachers having learned what they know. There is a clear benefit from being with someone who can pass on knowledge, especially someone who has previously been in the position of having to learn that knowledge. This latter qualification is a uniquely human characteristic. When a learner learns with an expert teacher, they are not simply gaining access to the teacher's knowledge but also benefiting from the teacher's memories of learning it themselves. Intelligent tutoring and adaptive learning systems can be programmed with pre-designated models of how something can be learned effectively. But no digital technology is going to 'learn' something exactly the way a human learns it, and then help another human learn accordingly.

Second is the capacity of human teachers to make cognitive connections. A human is uniquely placed to sense what another human is cognitively experiencing at any moment, and respond accordingly. In this sense, face-to-face contact with a teacher offers learners a valuable opportunity to engage in the process of thinking *with* another human brain. On the one hand, there is something thrilling about witnessing an expert who is modelling the process of thinking things through. Conversely, a human teacher is also able to make a personal 'cognitive connection' with another individual who is attempting to learn. As David Cohen puts it, teachers are uniquely able to 'put themselves into learners' mental shoes'.[11] Despite the best efforts of computer science, many aspects of thinking cannot be detected and modelled by machines in this way.

Third is the ability of human teachers to make social connections. Teaching involves a mutual obligation between teachers and learners. No teacher can stimulate the learning process without the cooperation of those who are learning. Good teachers make personal connections with their students, helping them gauge what might work best at any particular time. Before attempting to intellectually engage with a group, teachers will 'take a mental pulse of students' demeanors'.[12] Teachers work hard to establish this mutual commitment to learning, as well as sustaining engagement through motivating, cajoling and enthusing individual students. All of these are interpersonal skills that come naturally to people rather than any of the systems and applications outlined in this book.

Fourth is the unique ability of human teachers to think out loud. There is something transformative about being in the presence of an expert teacher talking about their subject of expertise. Listening to an expert talk can provide a real-time, unfolding connection with knowledge. A good speaker does not stick rigidly to a written text, but refines, augments and alters their argument according to the audience reactions. Any good teacher speaking to a group of learners therefore engages in a form of spontaneous revelation. Key to this is the teacher's role in leading and supporting learners to engage in active listening. As Gert Biesta reasons, being addressed by another person interrupts one's ego-centricism – drawing an individual out of themselves and forcing them into sense-making.[13]

A fifth quality – most apparent from Chapter 2's discussion of the limitations of physical robots – is the ability of human teachers to perform with their bodies. The bodies of human teachers are an invaluable resource when engaging learners in abstract thought. Teachers use their bodies to energize, orchestrate and anchor the performance of teaching. Many subtleties of teaching take place through movement, such as pacing around a room, pointing and gesturing. Teachers make use of their 'expressive body' – lowering their voice, raising an eyebrow or directing their gaze. Crucially, a human will respond to the living biological body of another human in a completely different way to even the most realistic simulation. To repeat a point made in Chapter 2, being looked in the eye by another person is a qualitatively different experience than being looked at by a 3D humanoid robot, let alone a 2D cartoon agent displayed on a screen.

Finally, there is the human teacher's ability to improvise and 'make do'. A key part of good teaching is the human capacity to improvise. Rather than sticking tightly to a pre-planned script, teachers will adjust what they do according to the circumstances. Like most performative events, any teaching session will involve a rough plan or structure. However, a good teacher will improvise their way around any pre-planned aims and objectives. Teaching requires acts of creativity, innovation and spontaneity – akin to dancing or playing jazz.[14] Teachers and learners feel each other out, find common ground and build upon it. Teaching also demands a tolerance for imprecision, messiness and not knowing. Most human actions involve a degree of guesswork, bluff and willingness to 'make do'. Even with an 'infinite supply of finite responses', these are processes that computer systems are ultimately incapable of.

Recognizing AI as a double-edged sword

Clearly, then, there are many sensible reasons to *not* anticipate the full 'robotization' of education any time soon. This is an area of exaggerated expectation and uninformed speculation. The capabilities of the technologies actually finding their way into education are far removed from descriptions of super-intelligent machines and the 'singularity'. Understandably, then, most sensible educators and other educational commentators like to reassure themselves that AI will never replace teachers. There are many aspects of teaching as a 'human improvement profession' that clearly require the central involvement of humans.

Yet this seemingly obvious conclusion highlights a significant impasse that is rarely mentioned in discussions of AI and education. Admittedly, it might well make good educational sense that human teachers can never be satisfactorily superseded by AI technology in ways that genuinely improve, enrich and enhance education. It is also certainly the case that many scientists, engineers and developers involved at the cutting-edge of the field readily acknowledge that they are a very long way off realizing the potential of these technologies. Nevertheless, there are plenty of people who are motivated to think and act otherwise. As Adam Greenfield puts it, 'the meaningful question isn't whether these technologies work as advertised. It's whether someone *believes* that they do, and acts on that belief.'[15] In this sense, the idea of 'robots replacing teachers' still needs to be treated as a serious proposition. While AI-driven teaching and learning might not make sense from an educational point of view, many people are still prepared to argue that it makes sense for a number of other reasons.

This relates back to this book's key concern of focusing on the politics of AI in education. Regardless of the clear limitations and compromises involved, there are a number of powerful interests arguing for the transformation of education through AI. In many cases, the idea of 'robots replacing teachers' is clearly being driven by wider ideals and ambitions to reform the nature of education – in other words, these are imperatives that are ideologically driven. In this sense, educational AI is a high-profile vehicle for advancing alternative visions of what education in the future might look like.

The ideological foundations of educational AI are wide-ranging and not necessarily consistent. For example, the development of intelligent tutoring systems, pedagogical agents and learning analytics seems often motivated by dissatisfactions with large-group classroom instruction. As noted in Chapter 1, a sense of techno-solutionism also pervades much current promotion of educational AI – that is, a naive belief that, 'given the right code, algorithms and robots, technology can solve all of mankind's problems, effectively making life "frictionless" and trouble-free'.[16] Also underpinning some arguments for educational AI are market-driven oppositions to mass compulsory public schooling, or libertarian suspicions of the state, or corporate opposition to the idea of organized labour. All these views may have their merits, but they are not necessarily grounded in the educational capabilities of the technology. In this sense, many of the AI systems and applications outlined in this book could be described as primarily acting as 'Trojan Horses' for broader concerns and bigger battles.

It is also important not to overlook the strong commercial imperatives underpinning the push for AI in education. As was noted at the beginning of Chapter 1, the global market for AI in education is expected to grow to around $3.7 billion by 2023. Alongside every small-scale university experiment with a few classroom robots, there are multinational corporations generating substantial profits from the automated grading of millions of standardized test assignments. This is not a field that is being driven by intellectual curiosity and a desire to build scientific knowledge. The educational applications of Sota and Jill Watson might appear to be genial and thought-provoking experiments, but there is also a lot of money to be made from the large-scale rollout of such innovations across school and university systems. These are not neutral technologies being developed for their own sake.

Scenario#1: AI as a prompt for less work?

Despite these 'bigger picture' concerns, it remains rare for educational AI to be discussed in terms of its politics and economics. Technology developers and the IT industry are focused primarily on designing and developing systems that 'work'. Conversely, most educators understandably find themselves caught up in the immediate challenges and complexities associated with teaching. Policymakers and managers are looking for possible fixes to the intractable problems inherent in running education systems. In short, the growing use of AI in education does not yet feature high enough on many people's priorities to be properly scrutinized or critiqued. Despite the concerns raised in this book, AI in education is still not seen as a particularly contentious issue amidst broader debates around education.

Indeed, AI tends to be anticipated (if at all) by educators in largely unproblematic ways. At best, these are technologies that are imagined as taking care of many of the 'routines', 'duties' and 'heavy lifting' associated with teaching.[17] As discussed in Chapter 4, it is presumed that teachers might be freed-up to engage in meaningful acts of leading, arranging, explaining and inspiring. Commentators such as Rose Luckin anticipate teachers having their own AI-driven 'assistants' – providing 'intelligent support for teachers' and 'reduc[ing] teacher stress and workload'. Such stories imply 'a future in which the role of the teacher continues to evolve and is eventually transformed; one where their time is used more effectively and efficiently, and where their expertise is better deployed, leveraged, and augmented'.[18]

This apolitical acceptance is not unique to education. There is a tendency across many sectors of work to presume that AI will eventually play out in uncomplicated terms as 'complementary' to human expertise – ultimately providing humans with opportunities to 'amplify and extend our capabilities'.[19] The idea of AI relieving people of hard work underpins popular enthusiasms for the eventual disappearance of 'dangerous, dirty and dull' tasks, and the long-term prospect of paying a universal basic income to people no longer required to work. More immediately, hopes of digital automation assisting rather than replacing workers abound in many areas of employment. Companies such as McDonald's claim that employees in their AI-driven restaurants are likely to take on 'value-added' roles instead of losing their jobs.[20] If fast-food workers have nothing to fear, then surely the same should also apply to teachers?

Scenario#2: AI as a prompt for worse work?

While reassuring for anyone currently working as a teacher, these expectations are clearly tone-deaf to the broader politics of contemporary education. As noted earlier, it is not the actual capabilities of AI technologies that are of primary importance here, but the social order that is being advanced through AI. In this sense, there is plenty of reason to expect the increased AI-driven automation of teaching to lead to the diminishment of teachers, teaching and education.

First, expectations of these technologies simply assisting teachers are highly contestable. As was argued in Chapter 4, there is a fine line between being assisted and being supervised. There is a similarly fine line between being guided and being directed. Clearly, the types of technology outlined in this book can be implemented for a variety of purposes. Regardless of the initial intentions of developers, the *actual* uses of these technologies in schools and universities will invariably be double-edged. A technology that records and analyses all conversations that take place between a teacher and their students *might* be used as a personal tool of reflective practice. However, it might *also* be used as an institutional tool of performance management. As noted throughout this book, contemporary education contexts are increasingly organized around performance management, measurements, metrics, auditing and accountability. If a device or application captures data about teachers and their teaching, then it is likely that data flows will extend well beyond the machine and individual teacher.

The idea of AI technology freeing teachers to work in more expansive ways is also questionable. In a practical sense, teachers are most likely to find themselves adjusting what they do in order to fit the expectations of the technology. This might take the form of speaking in ways that are most likely to be parsed by natural language processing, walking to areas of the classroom that are covered by sensors, or encouraging students to write in ways that will earn the approval of automated grading systems. Each of these might feel like modest adjustments, yet mean that teachers increasingly behave in ways that accommodate the limitations of the machines they are working with. Teachers having to work *like* robots is a far more likely scenario than their being replaced outright by robots.

In short, these are technologies that are most likely to control, deskill and demean the teachers they are assisting. They are systems and applications that inevitably detract from teachers' overall control of the work they are doing, while also undermining their professional judgement and expertise. Having control and autonomy over what one does is a key characteristic of dignified work. Making one's own decisions is a key element of exercising expert judgement. As Judy Wajcman contends, the 'proverbial elephant in the room' when talking about AI-led automation is that these technologies 'are facilitating not less work but more worse jobs'.[21] From this perspective, there are plenty of reasons to suspect that AI will *not* lead to the majority of teachers enjoying more meaningful work, or rich and humane interactions with their students and colleagues.

What next? AI as a chance to renegotiate education

So where now? The implementation of AI in education is not simply a case of 'take it or leave it'. We should not blithely accept these technologies in the hope that they will essentially leave things unchanged, or perhaps turn out to be a useful source of assistance. Yet neither should we reject AI technology outright. As Vincent Mosco reasons, 'even as the analog world remains important, there is no turning back from digital. Rather, we urgently need to advance citizen control over the core technologies, the data we generate, and how they are used.'[22] In this spirit, we need to 'think otherwise' about the technologies *and* the humans that are likely to populate the education systems of the future.

Clearly, this rethinking will be strengthened by a greater plurality of voices, opinions and interests. As argued in Chapter 1, agendas around AI and education have so far been dominated by technology designers and vendors, business interests and corporate reformers. There is a clear need for vigorous responses from educators, students, parents and other groups with a stake in public education. What do we *all* want from our education systems as AI-driven automation becomes more prominent across society? How can we broaden our imaginations and speculate about educational AI along different lines? This raises a number of suggestions in relation to our discussions so far.

First, AI technologies can certainly play a role in helping human teachers work *less* hard. Teachers would undoubtedly benefit from working fewer hours and being relieved of repetitive administrative and bureaucratic tasks. The challenge here is to develop forms of AI that allow teachers to withdraw from tasks and procedures that are of minimal educational value. AI should certainly be used to automate aspects of teaching work that deserve to be automated. Human teachers are limited in what they can do and in the time and energy that they have to do it. There are many mindless logistical and procedural tasks where keeping humans in the loop will slow things down. And there is certainly scope to reconfigure the teacher's role where such work is redistributed amongst machines. As Luciano Floridi puts it, 'we should make AI's stupidity work for human intelligence'.[23]

Second, there might be a benefit in educational AI striving to be more experimental and decidedly non-human. The real 'added value' of AI-based education might not lie in seeking to replicate biological and human ways of doing things. Instead, the greatest potential of AI might be realized in attempting to apply completely new sets of engineering principles to education. It is often argued that AI offers a prospect of developing processes that are uniquely computational in nature – bringing in maths and machines and 'stepping outside the human perspective altogether'.[24] Garry Kasparov reckoned that Big Blue defeated him by making chess moves that no human would think of making. This should be the central challenge to those wanting to develop new forms of AI-based education. If technology developers want an educational grand challenge or 'moonshot' opportunity, then they might attempt to show us a genuinely new way of doing things, rather than attempting to 'efficiently' replicate what is already being done.

Third, there are a number of fundamental ways in which AI should *not* be applied in education – most notably to synthesize human-like actions and processes. There are many aspects of education that are best carried out by expert human teachers in face-to-face contexts. As such, we need to create educational environments that allow human teachers to work in the embodied, creative, expressive and relational ways that only human teachers can. We need to develop educational settings that facilitate the expert things that teachers can do and that technology cannot. This implies spaces and times that realize the value of the human embodiment of knowledge, the unique experience of being in the presence of an expert human other, the human model-ling of thinking, and the social and affective bases of meaningful learning. These spaces should be collabo-rative, communal and cooperative. Education can be arranged in ways that allow human teaching to be rein-vented as a high-quality, dignified and empowered work – 'tak[ing] advantage of the uniquely human qualities of creativity, ideation and communication'.[25]

In short, then, these suggestions imply a number of contentions that are worth taking forward into future implementations of educational AI – a tentative 'Four Laws' of AI in education if you like:

- AI is *not* an imperative that education needs to adapt to, catch up with, or be reshaped around. Instead AI presents the education community with a series of choices and decisions. It is crucial that these choices and decisions are engaged with by as many people as possible.
- There are many important aspects of high-quality education that *cannot* be adequately calculated, predicted or modelled through AI technology. These characteristics alone necessitate continued investment in the teaching workforce, and support for the principle of employing well-trained, expert, professional human teachers.
- It makes no sense for education to reject AI technology outright – there is plenty of value in these developments. However, it is crucial that teachers work together with machines on their *own* terms – i.e. in ways that enhance, broaden and genuinely improve the quality and the nature of the education that results.
- Public, policy and professional debates about AI and education need to move on from concerns over getting AI to work like a human teacher. The

question, instead, should be about distinctly non-human forms of AI-driven technologies that could be imagined, planned and created for educational purposes.

Mostly, then, these statements point to the need to discuss and debate educational AI in far more nuanced ways than has been the case to date. There are a range of complex conversations that now need to take place in earnest. For example, educators need to speak forcibly and work to increase public understanding of the value of the human expert teacher. At the same time, teachers also need to be more conversant with the bigger issues inherent in the technologies that are being implemented in schools and universities. These conversations can be stimulated and supported through the establishment of education counterparts to the interdisciplinary research centres, think-tanks and lobby groups that are emerging to critically address the general rise of AI in society – such as the AI Now Institute and the Data & Society Institute in the US. At the same time, it is also important that these discussions are both long-term and localized. What is relevant for primary schools does not necessarily apply to higher education. Returning to our discussions in Chapter 2, what is relevant to Silicon Valley is likely to be different to what is deemed

important in Sapporo or Shanghai. Everyone in education needs to have a keen sense of how they can engage
critically with these issues and begin to push back.

Alongside this, technologists and developers need
to move beyond their own personal experiences of
teaching and learning, and become fully engaged with
the ethical, moral and political connotations of these
technologies when applied in education. This is especially pertinent to the application of AI technologies to
K12 schooling. The excuse of 'I'm just an engineer' is
not good enough.[26] To paraphrase Kate Crawford, if a
developer working in the area of education and technology knows everything about technology but nothing
about education, then they cannot be considered quali-
fied to do the job.[27]

Finally, there is a clear need for the IT industry and
'Big Tech' interests to significantly curtail the hubris
that seems to surround the implementation of their
products in education. Education is an area of society
that a lot of experts have been trying to 'fix' for decades.
As relative newcomers to this area, AI developers and
technologists would do well to take time to listen to and
learn from those involved in these previous efforts. At
the same time, the education community also needs to
talk more with technologists and industry – to initiate
discussions and explore areas of mutual concern and

collaboration. Above all, there is the need to foster realistic but expansive dialogue about the future of educational AI. As Zachary Lipton puts it: 'Making real progress in AI requires a public discourse that is sober and informed. Right now, the discourse is so completely unhinged it's impossible to tell what's important and what's not.'[28]

Conclusions

This book opened with a quotation from John Dewey – a twentieth-century philosopher beloved of educators but perhaps less familiar to technologists. Dewey warned against setting out to 'teach today's students as we taught yesterday's'. This advice continues to resonate eighty years after Dewey offered it. As the 2020s progress, most people would agree on the need to keep exploring ways in which education might be improved and updated. As such, it is always worth reconsidering and re-evaluating the nature of teachers and teaching. Human teachers are by no means perfect, and there will always be room to do better.

Nevertheless, these five chapters have also raised a range of other perspectives (including a few from Dewey) that warn against deploying new technologies and innovations without sound educational and societal justification. A strong argument can be made for education remaining an essentially human process. While teaching and learning should not be kept shackled to the past, there is much about robotics and AI in the classroom that is cause for alarm rather than celebration.

It therefore seems sensible to end this book on a balanced note. Of course, it is foolish to presume that teaching is *not* going to change at all in light of the powerful automated technologies that are now being developed. Yet it is equally foolish to imagine that these technologies are ready substitutes for human-led education provision. While today's educators cannot afford to rest easy, neither should they feel the need to accept change for change's sake. The most appropriate conclusion to this book, then, is to resist a definite answer to the question of 'Should Robots Replace Teachers?' Instead, the title of the book is best seen as a provocation. There is a lot more to the topic of automated education that needs to be discussed.

So, instead of a neat 'Yes/No' response we should finish with a call for further conversation. Teachers, technologists and anyone else with a stake in the future of education need to get together to collectively reimagine what 'the teacher' should be in an age of (semi-) intelligent machines. This is not a matter of arguing whether AI technologies are somehow 'better' or not than humans. Indeed, we would do well to move away from talking about technology in terms of working for *or* against humans. Technology is not simply something that humans work with. Instead, technology is entwined with the politics of determining what education is, and what sort of education we want for our future societies.

These might seem unsatisfactory points to conclude on – especially with regard to technology that is usually promoted in bold, decisive and transformative terms. Yet, hopefully, these five chapters have gone some way to mapping out the salient issues and the directions that such debates might take. While this book has not provided any definite answers, it has developed a host of more informed and pointed questions than we started with. Being clearer in what we are talking about (and why we need to continue these conversations) is an important first step in achieving meaningful and sustainable change. To conclude with another eighty-year-old observation from John Dewey, 'a problem well put is half solved'.

Preface

1 Judy Wajcman, 'Automation: is it really different this time?', *The British Journal of Sociology* 68:1 (2017): 126.

1 AI, Robotics and the Automation of Teaching

1 Adrian Mackenzie, *Machine Learners*, Cambridge MA: MIT Press, 2017.

2 Lee Gomes, 'Neuromorphic chips are destined for deep learning – or obscurity', *IEEE Spectrum*, 29 May 2017, https://spectrum.ieee.org/semiconductors/design/neuromorphic-chips-are-destined-for-deep-learningor-obscurity.

3 Andrew Ng, 'Why deep learning is a mandate for humans, not just machines', *Wired*, May 2015, www.wired.com/brandlab/2015/05/andrew-ng-deep-learning-mandate-humans-not-just-machines.

4 Sara Wachter-Boettcher, *Technically Wrong*, New York: W. W. Norton & Company, 2017.

5 Virginia Eubanks, *Automating Inequality*, New York: St. Martin's Press, 2018.

6 Larry Smar, cited in M. Bowden, 'The measured man', *The Atlantic*, May/June 2012, www.theatlantic.com/magazine/archive/2012/07/the-measured-man/309018.

7 Garry Kasparov, 'Robots will uplift us', *The Australian*, 24 May 2018, www.theaustralian.com.au.

8 Ann Ward, *Socrates and Dionysus*, Newcastle-upon-Tyne: Cambridge Scholars, 2014.

9 Terry Sejnowski, 'Artificial intelligence will make you smarter', *Edge*, 2015, www.edge.org/response-detail/26087.

10 David Cohen, *Teaching and its Predicaments*, Cambridge MA: Harvard University Press, 2011.

11 Market Report, *AI in Education*, 2018, www.marketsandmarkets. com/Market-Reports/ai-in-education-market-200371366.html.

12 Sejnowski, 'Artificial intelligence will make you smarter'.

13 Beverly Woolf, Chad Lane, Vinay Chaudhri and Janet Kolodner, 'AI grand challenges for education', *AI Magazine* 34:4 (2013): 66.

14 Anthony Seldon, cited in Henry Bodkin, '"Inspirational" robots to begin replacing teachers within 10 years', *Daily Telegraph*, 11 September 2017, www.telegraph.co.uk/science/2017/09/11/ inspirational-robots-begin-replacing-teachers-within-10-years.

15 Rose Luckin, Wayne Holmes, Mark Griffiths and Laurie Forcier, *Intelligence Unleashed*, London: Pearson, 2016.

16 Donald Clark, 'Could AI replace teachers? 10 ways it could?', *Plan B* blog, 4 July 2016, http://donaldclarkplanb.blogspot. com/2016/07/could-ai-replace-teachers-10-ways-it_4.html.

17 Kristin Houser, 'The solution to our education crisis might be AI', *Futurism*, 11 December 2017, https://futurism.com/ai-teachers-education-crisis.

18 Evgeny Morozov, *To Save Everything, Click Here*, New York: Public Affairs, 2013.

19 Bryan Caplan, *The Case Against Education*, Princeton: Princeton University Press, 2018.

20 Richard Susskind and Daniel Susskind, *The Future of the Professions*, Oxford: Oxford University Press, 2015.

21 Harry Collins, *Artifictional Intelligence*, Cambridge: Polity, 2018.

22 Wajcman, 'Automation: is it really different this time?', p. 119.

2 Physical Robots in the Classroom

1 Omar Mubin, Catherine Stevens, Suleman Shahid, Abdullah Al Mahmud and Jian-Jie Dong, 'A review of the applicability of robots in education', *Journal of Technology in Education and Learning* 1 (2013),#209-0015,http://roila.org/wp-content/uploads/2013/07/209-0015.pdf.

2 Jenay Beer, Arthur Fisk and Wendy Rogers, 'Toward a framework for levels of robot autonomy in human-robot interaction', *Journal of Human–Robot Interaction* 3:2 (2014): 74–99.

3 Sofia Serholt, Wolmet Barendregt, Asimina Vasalou, Patrícia Alves-Oliveira, Aidan Jones, Sofia Petisca and Ana Paiva, 'The case of classroom robots', *AI & Society* 32:4 (2017): 613.

4 Tsuyoshi Komatsubara, Masahiro Shiomi, Thomas Kaczmarek, Takayuki Kanda and Hiroshi Ishiguro, 'Estimating children's social status through their interaction activities in classrooms with a social robot', *International Journal of Social Robotics*, published online 27 March 2018.

5 Jeonghye Han, 'Emerging technologies: Robot assisted language learning', *Language Learning & Technology* 16:3 (2012): 1–9.

6 Mubin et al., 'A review of the applicability of robots in education'.

7 Ibid.

8 Hashimoto Takuya, Naoki Kato and Hiroshi Kobayashi, 'Development of educational system with the android robot SAYA and evaluation', *International Journal of Advanced Robotic Systems* 8:3 (2011): 52.

9 Hiroshi Kobayashi, cited in John Crace, 'Who needs teachers when you could have bankers? Or better still, robots?', *Guardian*, 13 March 2009, www.theguardian.com/education/mortarboard/2009/mar/13/robot-teacher-tokyo.

10 Bosede Edwards and Adrian Cheok, 'Why not robot teachers: Artificial Intelligence for addressing teacher shortage', *Applied Artificial Intelligence* 32:4 (2018): 345–60.

11 Cynthia Breazeal, 'Toward sociable robots', *Robotics and Autonomous Systems* 42:3–4 (2003): 167–75.

12 Takayuki Kanda, Takayuki Hirano, Daniel Eaton and Hiroshi Ishiguro, 'Interactive robots as social partners and peer tutors for children', *Human–Computer Interaction* 19:1–2 (2004): 61.

13 Minoo Alemi, Ali Meghdari and Maryam Ghazisaedy, 'The impact of social robotics on L2 learners' anxiety and attitude in English vocabulary acquisition', *International Journal of Social Robotics* 7:4 (2015): 523–35.

14 Fumihide Tanaka, Kyosuke Isshiki, Fumiki Takahashi, Manabu Uekusa, Rumiko Sei and Kaname Hayashi, 'Pepper learns together with children', *Proceedings of the 15th IEEE-RAS International Conference on Humanoid Robots*, Seoul, Korea, November 2015, p. 271. See also Fumihide Tanaka, 'How not so smart robots can enhance education', *TEDxTsukuba*, www.youtube.com/watch?v= eBnqaFFvxRM.

15 Ester Ferrari, Ben Robins and Kerstein Dautenhahn, 'Therapeutic and educational objectives in robot assisted play for children with autism', in *Robot and Human Interactive Communication, 2009 RO-MAN*, IEEE, 2009, pp. 108–14.

16 Edwards and Cheok, 'Why not robot teachers', p. 349.

17 Leopoldina Fortunati, 'Robotization and the domestic sphere', *New Media & Society* 20:8 (2018): 2673–90; Serholt et al., 'The case of classroom robots'.

18 Mubin et al., 'A review of the applicability of robots in education'.

19 Larry Cuban, *Teachers and Machines*, New York: Teachers College Press, 1986.

20 Amanda Sharkey, 'Should we welcome robot teachers?', *Ethics and Information Technology* 18:4 (2016): 283–97.

21 Ibid., p. 294.

22 Marcel Mauss, 'Techniques of the body', *Economy and Society* 2:1 (1973): 75.

23 Lawrence Hass, cited in Bill Green and Nick Hopwood, 'The body in professional practice, learning and education', in Bill Green and Nick Hopwood (eds), *The Body in Professional Practice, Learning and Education*, Berlin: Springer, 2015, pp. 15–33.

24 Sofia Serholt, 'Breakdowns in children's interactions with a robotic tutor', *Computers in Human Behavior* 81 (2018): 250–64.

25 Christoph Bartneck, Dana Kulić, Elizabeth Croft and Susana Zoghbi, 'Measurement instruments for the anthropomorphism, animacy, likeability, perceived intelligence, and perceived safety of robots', *International Journal of Social Robotics* 1:1 (2009): 71–81.

26 Anna-Lisa Vollmer, Robin Read, Dries Trippas and Tony Belpaeme, 'Children conform, adults resist', *Science Robotics* 3:21 (2018): eaat7111.

27 Sherry Turkle, *Alone Together*, New York: Basic Books, 2011.

28 Stef Aupers, 'The revenge of the machines', *Asian Journal of Social Science* 30:2 (2002): 199–220.

3 Intelligent Tutoring and Pedagogical Assistants

1 Noah Schroeder, Olusola Adesope and Rachel Gilbert, 'How effective are pedagogical agents for learning?', *Journal of Educational Computing Research* 49:1 (2013): 1.

2 William Swartout, Ron Artstein, Eric Forbell, Susan Foutz, Chad Lane, Belinda Lange, Jacquelyn Ford Morie, Albert Rizzo and David Traum, 'Virtual humans for learning', *AI Magazine* 34:4 (2013): 13.

3 Patrick Suppes, 'Observations about the application of artificial intelligence research to education', in D. Walker and R. Hess (eds), *Instructional Software*, Belmont CA: Wadsworth, 1984, p. 306.

4 Abigail Gertner and Kurt VanLehn, 'Andes: a coached problem solving environment for physics', in *International Conference on Intelligent Tutoring Systems*, Berlin: Springer, 2000, pp. 133–42.

5 Swartout et al., 'Virtual humans for learning', p. 13.

6 Geraldine Clarebout and Steffi Heidig, 'Pedagogical agents', in *Encyclopedia of the Sciences of Learning*, Berlin: Springer, 2012, p. 2569.

7 James Lester, Charles Callaway, Joël Grégoire, Gary Stelling, Stuart Towns and Luke Zettlemoyer, 'Animated pedagogical agents in knowledge-based learning environments', in Kenneth D. Forbus and Paul J. Feltovich (eds), *Smart Machines in Education*, Cambridge MA: MIT Press, 2001, pp. 269–98.

8 Mark Lepper, Michael Drake and Teresa O'Donnell-Johnson, 'Scaffolding techniques of expert human tutors', in K. Hogan and M. Pressley (eds), *Scaffolding Student Learning*, New York: Brookline, 1997, p. 108.

9 Art Graesser, Mark Conley and Andrew Olney, 'Intelligent tutoring systems', in S. Graham and K. Harris (eds), *APA Handbook of Educational Psychology*, Washington DC: American Psychological Association, 2009, p. 182.

10 Stan Franklin and Art Graesser, 'Is it an agent, or just a program?', in *International Workshop on Agent Theories, Architectures, and Languages*, Berlin: Springer, 1996, pp. 21–35.

11 Clarebout and Heidig, 'Pedagogical agents', p. 2569.

12 Lewis Johnson and Jeff Rickel, 'Steve: an animated pedagogical agent for procedural training in virtual environments', *ACM SIGART Bulletin* 8:1–4 (1997): 16–21.

13 Swartout et al., 'Virtual humans for learning', p. 14.

14 Yangee Kim and Amy Baylor, 'Research-based design of pedagogical agent roles', *International Journal of Artificial Intelligence in Education* 26:1 (2016): 166.

15 See www.alelo.com/enskill.

16 Sidney D'Mello, Tanner Jackson, Scotty Craig, Brent Morgan, Patrick Chipman, Holly White and Natalie Person, 'AutoTutor detects and responds to learners' affective and cognitive states', in *Workshop on Emotional and Cognitive Issues at the International Conference on Intelligent Tutoring Systems*, Rotterdam: Springer, 2008, pp. 306–8.

17 Kim and Baylor, 'Research-based design of pedagogical agent roles'.

18 David Traum, Comments to American Educational Research Association annual meeting, New York, April 2018.

19 Lewis Johnson and James Lester, 'Face-to-face interaction with pedagogical agents, twenty years later', *International Journal of Artificial Intelligence in Education* 26:1 (2016): 25–36.

20 Kim and Baylor, 'Research-based design of pedagogical agent roles'.

21 Ning Wang, Ari Shapiro, Andrew Feng, Cindy Zhuang, Chirag Merchant, David Schwartz and Stephen Goldberg, 'Learning by explaining to a digital doppelganger', in *International Conference on Intelligent Tutoring Systems*, Berlin: Springer, 2018, pp. 256–64.

22 Beverly Woolf et al., 'AI grand challenges for education'.

23 Johnson and Lester, 'Face-to-face interaction with pedagogical agents', p. 34.

24 Swartout et al., 'Virtual humans for learning', p. 13.

25 George Veletsianos and Charles Miller, 'Conversing with pedagogical agents', *British Journal of Educational Technology* 39:6 (2008): 969–86.

26 William Lester and Art Graesser, Comments to American Educational Research Association annual meeting, New York, April 2018.

27 Art Graesser, Comments to American Educational Research Association annual meeting, New York, April 2018.

28 Schroeder et al., 'How effective are pedagogical agents for learning?', p. 1.

29 Johnson and Lester, 'Face-to-face interaction with pedagogical agents'.

30 Ibid., p. 31.

31 Art Graesser, 'Instruction based on tutoring', in Richard Mayer and Patricia Alexander (eds), *Handbook of Research on Learning and Instruction*, London: Routledge, 2011, pp. 410–11.

32 Vito Campanelli, Francesco Bardo and Nicole Heber, *Web Aesthetics*, Rotterdam: NAi Publishers, 2010, p. 92.

33 Ibid., p. 94.

34 Audrey Watters, 'Education technology and the new behaviorism', *Hack Education* blog, 23 December 2017, http://hackeducation.com/2017/12/23/top-ed-tech-trends-social-emotional-learning.

35 Rupert Alcock, 'What the mainstreaming of behavioural nudges reveals about neoliberal government', *The Conversation*, 17 October 2017, https://theconversation.com/what-the-mainstreaming-of-behavioural-nudges-reveals-about-neoliberal-government-85580.

36 Nick Seaver, 'Captivating algorithms', *Journal of Material Culture* (forthcoming 2019).

4 'Behind-the-Scenes' Technologies

1 B. F. Skinner, *The Technology of Teaching*, New York: Appleton-Century-Crofts, 1968, p. 27.

2 Bill Ferster, *Teaching Machines*, Baltimore: Johns Hopkins University Press, 2014.

3 Rob Kitchin, *The Data Revolution*, London: Sage, 2014.

4 Anna Wilson, Cate Watson, Terrie Lynn Thompson, Valerie Drew and Sarah Doyle, 'Learning analytics: challenges and limitations', *Teaching in Higher Education* 22:8 (2017): 991–1000.

5 Rebecca Ferguson, 'Learning analytics', *International Journal of Technology Enhanced Learning* 4:5–6 (2012): 304–17.

6 Roberto Martinez-Maldonado, Vanessa Echeverria, Olga Santos, Augusto Dias Pereira Dos Santos and Kalina Yacef, 'Physical learning analytics', in *Proceedings of the 8th International Conference on Learning Analytics and Knowledge*, Rotterdam: Springer, 2018, pp. 375–9.

7 Lizzie Palmer, 'Eton for all', *New Statesman*, 2 October 2017, www.newstatesman.com/politics/education/2017/10/eton-all-will-robot-teachers-mean-everyone-gets-elite-education.

8 Peter Foltz, 'Advances in automated scoring of writing for performance assessment', in *Handbook of Research on Technology Tools for Real-world Skill Development*, Hershey PA: IGI Global, 2016, pp. 659–78.

9 Tovia Smith, 'More states opting to "robo-grade" student essays by computer', *NPR Weekend Edition*, 30 June 2018, www.npr.org/2018/06/30/624373367/more-states-opting-to-robo-grade-student-essays-by-computer.

10 B. F. Skinner, 'Teaching machines', *Science* 128:3330 (1958): 976.

11 Abelardo Pardo, 'Feedback is good, but scaling it. . .', *BERA* blog, 13 July 2018, www.bera.ac.uk/blog/feedback-is-good-but-scaling-it.

12 Anthony Seldon, cited in Palmer, 'Eton for all'.

13 Lee Rainie and Barry Wellman, *Networked*, Cambridge MA: MIT Press, 2011.

14 Harry Braverman, *Labour and Monopoly Capital*, New York: Monthly Review Press, 1974.

15 Audrey Watters, 'The weaponization of education data', *Hack Education* blog, 11 December 2017, http://hackeducation.com/2017/12/11/top-ed-tech-trends-weaponized-data.

5 Revitalizing Teaching for the AI Age

1 Paul Virillo, *Politics of the Very Worst*, New York: Semiotext(e), 1999, p. 89.

2 Nick Couldry, https://twitter.com/couldrynick/status/98478187
   3523118081.

3 Alexander Galloway, 'The golden age of analog (it's now)',
   Presentation to Penn School of Social Policy and Practice, 2 October
   2017, www.youtube.com/watch?v=bpArIaBdEf8.

4 Murray Goulden, https://twitter.com/murraygoulden/status/103
   8338924270297094.

5 Adam Greenfield, *Radical Technologies*, London: Verso, 2017,
   p. 249.

6 Jonas Ivarsson, 'Algorithmic accountability', *Lärande | Learning &
   IT* blog, 2 May 2017, http://lit.blogg.gu.se/2017/05/02/algorith
   mic-accountability.

7 Hubert L. Dreyfus, *Alchemy and Artificial Intelligence*, Santa Monica
   CA: RAND Corporation, 1965, www.rand.org/content/dam/rand/
   pubs/papers/2006/P3244.pdf.

8 J. Kay, 'Scrutable adaptation', in *International Conference on Adaptive Hypermedia and Adaptive Web-Based Systems*, Berlin: Springer,
   2006, pp. 11–19.

9 Hilary Mason, https://twitter.com/hmason/status/101418060649
   6968704.

10 Edsger Dijkstra, cited in Robert Boyer, 'In memoriam: Edsger
   W. Dijkstra', *Communications of the ACM* 45:10 (2002):
   21–2.

11 Cohen, *Teaching and its Predicaments*, p. 177.

12 Beth Bernstein-Yamashiro and Gil Noam, 'Teacher:student
   relationships', *New Directions for Youth Development*, Spring 2013,
   p. 4.

13 Gert Biesta, 'The rediscovery of teaching', *Educational Philosophy
   and Theory* 48:4 (2016): 374–92.

14 Carol Ann Tomlinson and Amy Germundson, 'Teaching as jazz',
   Educating the Whole Child 64:8 (2007): 27–31.

15 Greenfield, *Radical Technologies*, p. 243.

16 Ian Tucker, 'Interview with Evgeny Morozov: We are abandoning all the checks and balances', *Guardian*, 9 March 2013, www.the guardian.com/technology/2013/mar/09/evgeny-morozov-technol ogy-solutionism-interview.

17 James Manyika, *A Future that Works*, New York: McKinsey & Company, 2017. Manyika talks of 'routines', Edwards and Cheok ('Why not robot teachers') talk of duties, while Seldon (cited in Bodkin, '"Inspirational" robots') evokes 'heavy lifting'.

18 Luckin et al., *Intelligence Unleashed*, p. 11.

19 Sarah Bergbreiter cited in SingularityU, https://twitter.com/ SingularityU_AU/status/965728520440696832.

20 Greenfield, *Radical Technologies*, p. 195.

21 Wajcman, 'Automation: is it really different this time?', p. 124.

22 Vincent Mosco, *Becoming Digital*, Bingley: Emerald, 2017, p. 6.

23 Luciano Floridi, 'Should we be afraid of AI?', *Aeon*, 9 May 2016, https://aeon.co/essays/true-ai-is-both-logically-possible-and-utterly-implausible.

24 Murray Shanahan, *The Technological Singularity*, Cambridge MA: MIT Press, 2015, p. xxii.

25 Wajcman, 'Automation: is it really different this time?', p. 124.

26 Ramesh Srinivasan, 'We, the users', Presentation to Alan Turing Institute, June 2018, www.youtube.com/watch?v=Of8NAP-1X0c.

27 See https://twitter.com/katecrawford.

28 Zachary Lipton, cited in Oscar Schwartz, '"The discourse is unhinged": how the media gets AI alarmingly wrong', *Guardian*, 25 July 2018, www.theguardian.com/technology/2018/jul/25/ai-arti ficial-intelligence-social-media-bots-wrong.

Index

WILEY END USER LICENSE AGREEMENT